W9-AUK-553

Native Cultures in Alaska

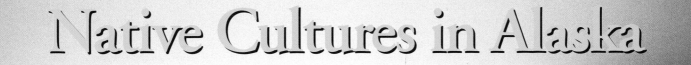

ALASKA GEOGRAPHIC Volume 23, Number 2

To teach many more to better know and more wisely use our natural resources...

EDITOR
Penny Rennick

PRODUCTION DIRECTOR
Kathy Doogan

STAFF WRITER
L.J. Campbell

MARKETING MANAGER
Pattey Parker Mancini

CIRCULATION/DATABASE MANAGER
Linda Flowers

BOARD OF DIRECTORS
Richard Carlson
Kathy Doogan
Penny Rennick

Robert A. Henning, President Emeritus

POSTMASTER: Send address changes to:

ALASKA GEOGRAPHIC®
P.O. Box 93370
Anchorage, Alaska 99509-3370

PRINTED IN KOREA

ISBN: 1-56661-031-1

COVER: *Tlingit carver Nathan Jackson works in Saxman on a Raven house post for the Eiteljorg Museum of American Indians and Western Art in Indianapolis, Ind. (Hall Anderson)*

PREVIOUS PAGE: *An Inupiat whaling crew from Barrow, led by Capt. Ben Itta, lands a bowhead. (Henry P. Huntington)*

FACING PAGE: *Angela Odinzoff gathers grass for basket making in the Yup'ik village of Stebbins. (Roz Goodman)*

ABOUT THIS ISSUE: This issue is intended to help readers better understand the cultural richness and diversity of Alaska's indigenous people. While not meant to be comprehensive, it provides glimpses of what it means to be Alaska Native today.

Numerous Alaska Natives helped with this effort. Invaluable were contributions by Barbara Švarný Carlson, Gordon Pullar, Anecia Lomack, Sheila Frankson, Velma Wallis and Nathan Jackson. Our sincere thanks to each of them.

The remainder of the issue was written by L.J. Campbell, who also served as project editor. She thanks the many people who granted interviews and shared experiences and insights for background as well as attribution. She also thanks the other *ALASKA GEOGRAPHIC®* staffers, particularly Penny Rennick and Kathy Doogan, for their support.

We appreciate the photographers who brought faces and activities of Alaska Natives to these pages, submitting many more fine images than could possibly be included.

In addition, we thank the following people who provided information and reviewed portions of the text: Michael Krauss, director, Alaska Native Language Center; Aron Crowell, director, Smithsonian Institution's Arctic Studies Center in Anchorage; Abraham Friendly, adjunct instructor Central Yup'ik language and culture, University of Alaska Anchorage; archaeologist Rick Knecht, museum project director, City of Unalaska; Joe Kelley, Kodiak Area Native Association; John F.C. Johnson, director, Chugach Heritage Foundation; Wallace Olson, professor of anthropology emeritus, University of Alaska Southeast; Richard Dauenhauer, Sealaska Heritage Foundation; Amy Van Hatten, Athabaskan coordinator, Alaska Rural Systemic Initiative; Bill Simeone, Alaska Dept. of Fish and Game; Will Mayo, president, Tanana Chiefs Conference Inc.; Henry P. Huntington, Inuit Circumpolar Conference; Marie Adams and Elise Patkotak, Public Information Office, North Slope Borough; Elmer Goodwin, Northwest Alaska Native Association; archaeologist Chris Wooley, Anchorage.

Thanks also to many others who helped in various ways, including: Cecilia Martz; Debbie Bourdokofsky; Linda DeWitt; Teri Rofkar; Min Bartels; Roby Littlefield; Mike Jackson; Ethan Pettigrew; teacher and Aleut linquist Moses Dirks of Anchorage; Sue Thorsen with Sitka National Historical Park; Andy Hope, Alaska Rural Systemic Initiative; and Linda Cook, National Park Service, Alaska Region.

Contributor Barbara Švarný Carlson would like to acknowledge: Nick Galaktionoff, Sophie Sherebernikoff, Platonida Gromoff, Neon Merculieff, Moses Gordieff, Peat Galaktionoff, Walter Dyakanoff, Knut Bergsland, Moses Dirks, Wendy Švarný-Hawthorne, Diane Švarný and Ray Hudson.

Population figures came from the 1990 census, the 1995 census update, or from local governments. The numbers of Native speakers are from the Alaska Native Language Center. □

ALASKA GEOGRAPHIC® (ISSN 0361-1353) is published quarterly by The Alaska Geographic Society, 639 West International Airport Road, Unit 38, Anchorage, AK 99518. Periodicals postage paid at Anchorage, Alaska, and additional mailing offices.

Copyright © 1996 by The Alaska Geographic Society. All rights reserved. Registered trademark: Alaska Geographic, ISSN 0361-1353; Key title Alaska Geographic.

THE ALASKA GEOGRAPHIC SOCIETY is a non-profit, educational organization dedicated to improving geographic understanding of Alaska and the North, putting geography back in the classroom and exploring new methods of teaching and learning.

SOCIETY MEMBERS RECEIVE *ALASKA GEOGRAPHIC®*, a high-quality, full-color quarterly that devotes each issue to monographic, in-depth coverage of a northern region or resource-oriented subject. Back issues are also available. For current membership rates, or to order or request a free catalog of back issues, contact: The Alaska Geographic Society, P.O. Box 93370, Anchorage, AK 99509-3370; phone (907) 562-0164, fax (907) 562-0479

SUBMITTING PHOTOGRAPHS: Those interested in submitting photographs should write for a list of upcoming topics or other specific photo needs and a copy of our editorial guidelines. We cannot be responsible for unsolicited submissions. Submissions not accompanied by sufficient postage for return by certified mail will be returned by regular mail.

CHANGE OF ADDRESS: The post office does not automatically forward *ALASKA GEOGRAPHIC®* when you move. To ensure continuous service, please notify us at least six weeks before moving. Send your new address and membership number or a mailing label from a recent *ALASKA GEOGRAPHIC®* to: Alaska Geographic Society, Box 93370, Anchorage, AK 99509. If your book is returned to us by the post office, we will contact you to ask if you wish to receive a replacement for $5 (for postage charges).

COLOR SEPARATIONS: Graphic Chromatics

The Library of Congress has cataloged this serial publication as follows:

Alaska Geographic. v.1-
    [Anchorage, Alaska Geographic Society] 1972-
    v. ill. (part col.). 23 x 31 cm.
    Quarterly
    Official publication of The Alaska Geographic Society.
    Key title: Alaska geographic, ISSN 0361-1353.

    1. Alaska—Description and travel—1959-
    —Periodicals. I. Alaska Geographic Society.

F901.A266 917.98'04'505 72-92087

Library of Congress 75[79112] MARC-S.

Contents

Introduction

The first people to North America arrived many thousands of years ago. Today, many of their descendants still live in Alaska — people collectively known as Alaska Natives.

Alaska Natives are a political force with certain rights and privileges. They share a common history of events that have shaped their modern existence. They are the only indigenous people in the United States who haven't been relocated to reservations by the federal government, with the exception of the Tsimshians of Metlakatla, who requested reservation status. All other Alaska Natives still live, hunt and fish on the lands of their ancestors. Many Alaska Natives still speak their ancestral languages, perform ancestral dances, tell ancestral stories and practice age-old values handed down through generations.

But they also are members of the modern world. Many hold the jobs, embrace the technology and use the tools of a global economy. They struggle with many of the same problems as their non-Native neighbors, but increasingly are looking within their cultures for solutions. As Elders age and the body of traditional knowledge grows dimmer, maturing generations face new challenges in continuing their heritage.

Even so, Alaska Natives are not a single, homogeneous entity. Broadly identified as Aleuts, Eskimos and Indians, the people who are Alaska Natives belong, more specifically, to one of 20 language and culture groups. Within those, they have particular village and tribal affiliations. Each group identifies a different geographic region where their ancestors lived and where their home villages are today.

The Native cultures in Alaska are:

Aleut or *Unangax̂*: The Aleutian and Pribilof islands and southern Alaska Peninsula

Alutiiq: The Kodiak Island archipelago, Alaska Peninsula, Lower Cook Inlet and Prince William Sound

Yup'ik: Southwest and the Bering Sea coast

Siberian Yupik: St. Lawrence Island

Inupiat: Northwest and Arctic

Athabaskan (11 language groups): Interior and Southcentral

Eyak: Cordova and Yakutat

Tlingit: Southeast

Tsimshian: Metlakatla in Southeast

Haida: Southern Southeast

This issue takes a closer look at the rich and diverse cultures of Alaska's various Native groups, and how they continue cultural practices and activities within the contexts of contemporary society. ■

FACING PAGE: *Nova Slye and John Baechler Jr. hang red salmon backbones to dry for dog feed at a homestead owned by Slye's Athabaskan grandmother, Rose Hedlund, at Chekok on Lake Iliamna. (Roz Goodman)*

Alaska's Native Cultures

In the evenings after work in Sitka, Min Bartels often goes to the beach to collect gumboots, or chitons, for her elderly aunt Ethel Makinen. In Barrow, Fannie Akpik spends an afternoon each week at the local radio station recording programs in Inupiaq for later broadcast. On Unalaska Island, Andrew Gronholt, an Aleut Elder originally from Unga, teaches the art of making bentwood hunting visors to school students and adults. In the Athabaskan village of Huslia, Catherine Attla tells stories in her Koyukon language that were told by her grandfather; her Native knowledge of the region is widely respected and she has served many years on state hunting and fishing advisory committees. From the docks in downtown Anchorage, Inupiat Percy Blatchford and his son, Joel, are among a number of urban Natives who drive their boats across Cook Inlet to go subsistence beluga whale hunting.

In Alaska's farthest reaches and in its largest cities, people are carrying on their Native ways.

They do so in thousands of variations of the old and new.

They hunt, fish and gather food to eat, connecting with the land for cultural reasons, as well as for nutritional and economic necessity. Those who do, share with those who can't. Even many with cash wage jobs find time to participate in this lifeline. Schools in many villages start early in fall to let out early in spring, so families can go fishing. "Subsistence is truly a way of life, from one season to the next," says Teri Rofkar, a Tlingit in Sitka. "It's not something you do separately. It's a part of you. A kind of important part for me."

Likewise, many Alaska Natives carve and weave, making tools, clothing and artworks in the fashion of those before them. They congregate for feasts to honor the dead and celebrate the living, using ancient words held in memory for those occasions. They sing old songs and write new ones. Sometimes their drums are still covered in the old way with animal intestines,

but today the heads are as likely to be made of nylon. In a pinch during a visit to Anchorage, a Yup'ik drummer accompanied himself on a plastic Frisbee with an old wooden kitchen spoon, for an impromptu session teaching dance and song to a friend's child.

Alaska Natives are not relics, stuck in a time-warp of the past. Their cultures are more than shards of pottery or shreds of basketry in museum cases. Alaska Native cultures are alive today in ways expected and unexpected. There are some common themes between culture

FACING PAGE: *As Wayne Price signals from the bench, about 200 people pulling on six ropes raise a 35-foot totem pole at Sitka National Historical Park in 1996. The pole, carved by Will Burkhart, Tommy Joseph and Price, is the first traditional totem raised by Sitka Tlingits in more than 100 years. (Jim Lavrakas,* Anchorage Daily News)

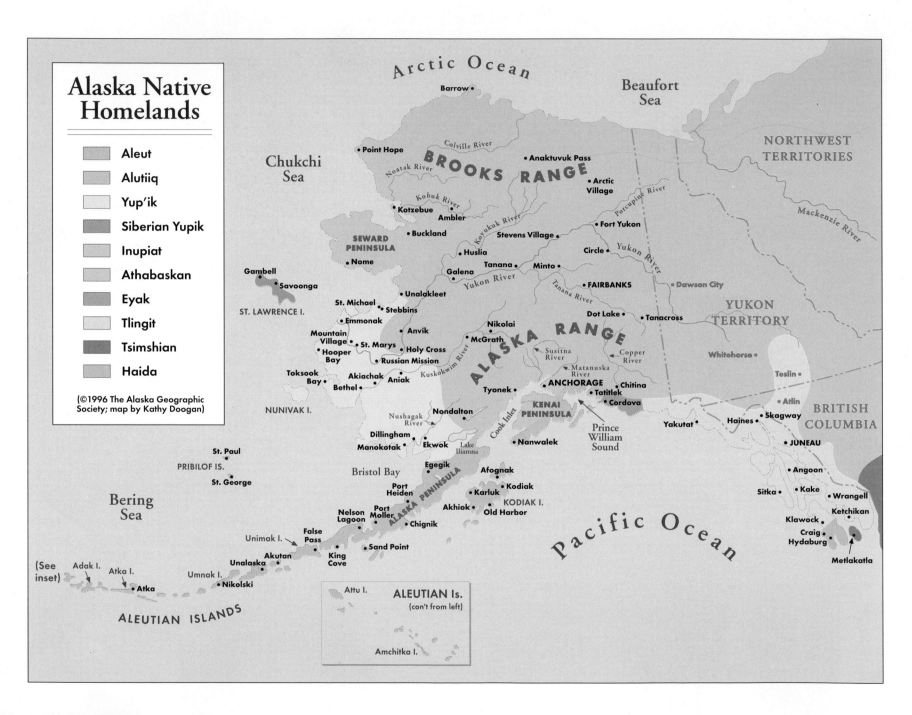

Alaska Native Homelands

Legend:
- Aleut
- Alutiiq
- Yup'ik
- Siberian Yupik
- Inupiat
- Athabaskan
- Eyak
- Tlingit
- Tsimshian
- Haida

(©1996 The Alaska Geographic Society; map by Kathy Doogan)

Arctic Ocean

Beaufort Sea

Chukchi Sea

NORTHWEST TERRITORIES

Barrow

Point Hope

Colville River

BROOKS RANGE

Anaktuvuk Pass

Arctic Village

Noatak River

Kobuk River

Porcupine River

Mackenzie River

Kotzebue
Ambler

Koyukuk River

Fort Yukon

SEWARD PENINSULA

Buckland

Stevens Village

Circle

Yukon River

Huslia

Tanana

Minto

DAWSON CITY area — Dawson City

Nome

Galena

YUKON TERRITORY

Gambell
Savoonga

Unalakleet

Yukon River

FAIRBANKS

ST. LAWRENCE I.

St. Michael
Stebbins

Tanana River

Dot Lake

Tanacross

Emmonak

Anvik

Nikolai

ALASKA RANGE

Whitehorse

Mountain Village
Hooper Bay

St. Marys

Holy Cross

McGrath

Susitna River

Copper River

Teslin

Russian Mission

Toksook Bay

Akiachak

Aniak

Kuskokwim River

Matanuska River

ANCHORAGE

Chitina

Atlin

BRITISH COLUMBIA

Bethel

Tyonek

Tatitlek
Cordova

NUNIVAK I.

Nushagak River

Nondalton

KENAI PENINSULA

Prince William Sound

Yakutat

Haines

Skagway

St. Paul

Dillingham

Ekwok

Lake Iliamna

Cook Inlet

Nanwalek

JUNEAU

PRIBILOF IS.

Manokotak

Bristol Bay

Egegik

Afognak

Angoon

St. George

Port Heiden

Kodiak

KODIAK I.

Sitka

Kake

Bering Sea

Nelson Lagoon

Port Moller

Karluk

Akhiok

Old Harbor

Wrangell

ALASKA PENINSULA

Chignik

Ketchikan

(See inset)

Adak I.

Atka I.

Umnak I.

Unalaska

Akutan

False Pass

King Cove

Sand Point

Klawock

Craig
Hydaburg

Atka

Nikolski

Unimak I.

Metlakatla

ALEUTIAN ISLANDS

Attu I.

ALEUTIAN Is.
(con't from left)

Amchitka I.

Pacific Ocean

LEFT: *Cynthia Jim of Angoon watches her bingo cards for the winning combination in a game several years ago. Bingo, regulated under the charitable gaming law as a way for nonprofits and municipalities to raise money, is a favorite pastime in many Alaska villages. (Don Pitcher)*

ABOVE: Jonathan John drives his father, Abraham John Sr., to subsistence hunt caribou in the mountains near Arctic Village, a Gwich'in Athabaskan settlement that depends on the Porcupine caribou herd. Abraham Sr. hunted regularly until his death in 1994. (George Matz)

groups, yet innumerable twists in the way circumstances and cultures combine. But as they have been throughout time, Alaska Natives are innovators, adapting old traditions and creating new ones, linking past with present in a continuum of their cultures. They are today's version of Alaska's original people.

The Beginnings

Alaska's original people occupied these northlands many thousands of years ago. Some Native stories recall the distant past, when people and animals shared the same language and could transform one to another. In Yup'ik cosmology, beings moved between realms during a time when "the earth was thin."

In more recent times, Alaska's people traveled across the land, along the coasts and up the rivers. Some stone tools found in Alaska in places where early people camped are 10,000 to 11,000 years old.

Archaeologists believe that North America's first people filtered from the land mass known today as Asia. They traveled in small bands at different times, as they hunted large mammals across the continent-sized land bridge connecting Siberia and Alaska. Ancient sites from this era have been found on the North Slope, in the Interior, in the Aleutian Islands and in Southeast. The tools found in these sites vary, indicating the existence of different cultures at similar times. Perhaps some early people even

boated along the coastlines. Archaeologists offer various scenarios about how these ancient people dispersed throughout Alaska and their relationships to each other and later arrivals.

Language Affinities

The early people included groups broadly defined as Paleoindians, NaDene and Eskaleut by linguists looking at language links and

ABOVE: *The blanket toss is a distinctive Inupiat tradition from days when hunters were tossed high to spot animals across the flat landscape.* (Chris Wooley)

RIGHT: *Siberian Yupik whale hunters sail after a bowhead in the Bering Sea off St. Lawrence Island. They make their strikes using walrus skin boats, although aluminum boats and motors may be used later in landing the whale.* (Chlaus Lotscher)

archaeologists looking at tool traditions. A simplistic portrait of their connections to today's Native cultures goes something like this: The Paleoindians, some of the earliest people, filtered through Alaska in a southerly migration to the lower continent. Later came the NaDene Indians, who were ancestors to Alaska's Athabaskans, Eyaks and Tlingits. The Eskaleut arrived even later and in their disparate movements developed into Alaska's Aleuts culture and its Eskimo groups — the Inupiat,

Yup'ik and Siberian Yupik — as well as, say linguists, the Alutiiq. The ancient links to the Haida and Tsimshian Indians are more obscure.

Of Alaska's population of 550,043 people in the 1990 census, Natives totalled 85,698, or 15.6 percent. This included 44,401 Eskimos (Inupiat, Yup'ik and Siberian Yupik); 31,245 American Indians (including 11,696 Athabaskans; 9,448 Tlingits; 1,083 Haida; 1,653 Tsimshian) and 10,052 Aleuts (including about 2,000 *Unangax̂* and about 3,000 Alutiiq in their home regions).

Survival Adaptations

Alaska's indigenous people developed ingenious ways to survive off the land and sea, using minerals and plant and animal materials for tools, clothing and shelter. They

were astute observers, reading their environment for clues to weather patterns and animal migrations. Many engaged in long-range trade through aboriginal networks. They developed complicated social structures and belief systems to govern individual actions and group activities, with undesirable consequences to those who became careless or offensive. People committed their personal and cultural histories to memory, along with their rules for behaving and living. All this vital information was passed on from generation to generation through examples and stories.

Contact

At the time of initial contact with outsiders — about 1741 when Danish Capt. Vitus Bering sailed through the North Pacific in his second exploring expedition for the Russian czar — northern North America was occupied by many Native groups, including those in Alaska today.

Prolonged contact with Westerners began at different times for Natives in different regions, from about 1750 along the southern coast through about 1870 in the more inland regions.

Explorers, fur traders, gold miners and missionaries were among the earliest outsiders. They brought different attitudes, values, foods, tools and customs. Alaska's various Native groups felt all these influences, some of which they willingly embraced, others which they didn't.

The newcomers inadvertently introduced foreign germs. Disease epidemics raged during the early years of contact, sometimes decimating villages and reducing Native populations to a fraction of their precontact strength.

The influx of outsiders changed how Natives used the land. Settlements and towns sprang up on traditional hunting, fishing and ceremonial grounds, and land transactions generally ignored territorial claims by Natives. Tlingits in Southeast tried to regain land as early as 1890, when Chief Johnson of the Taku tribe sued — albeit unsuccessfully — whites who built a dock in Juneau on his property.

Among the early influences that had long-lived effects were missionaries and educational policies. After Russia sold Alaska to the U.S. government in 1867, Alaska Natives fell under the law for a time as "uncivilized tribes." General agent of education Sheldon Jackson divided Alaska among various religious denominations, which established missions and schools to give the Native children a Christian upbringing and education. Many Native people today worship in the faith that converted their parents and grandparents. The missionaries also curtailed many traditional Native ceremonies, practically to extinction in some places. Although some of the earliest missionaries developed written alphabets for Native languages and translated

LEFT: *During the* Quiana *festival in Anchorage, dancers from Hooper Bay perform a masked dance from the ceremonial "Bladder Festival" that celebrates a young man's taking of his first seal. Such masked dances had been subject to repression early this century, but in recent years Elders and others have been reviving these traditions. (Barbara Willard)*

BELOW: *Marie Paneak roasts caribou at a fall hunting camp on Ekokpuk Creek near the Inupiat village of Anaktuvuk Pass. (Henry P. Huntington)*

church writings, the preachers and government teachers who came later insisted that the Native children learn and speak only English in the schools, often punishing them if they forgot. In 1972, a law passed requiring bilingual education in many of the schools.

For many years, Natives were treated as second-class citizens, made to attend separate

Luci Ivanoff fishes for tomcod at the mouth of the Unalakleet River in mid-November. (Roz Goodman)

schools and restaurants and to sit in the rear rows of theaters. In 1945, Alaska's territorial legislature finally passed a nondiscrimination act—the nation's first—that required businesses to remove signs banning Native trade.

The 1940s, '50s and '60s quickened the pace of change. World War II brought the military to Alaska. Many Native men served during the war and afterward found jobs building and maintaining military facilities in rural Alaska. In societies that valued self-reliance and hunting prowess, more men found themselves juggling cash wage employment

with subsistence activities. Women likewise were adjusting their roles and activities as they faced changing economic, educational and religious values. With the proliferation of Western ways, young Natives had a confusing range of role models.

Some individuals denied their Nativeness to function easier in the dominant society. Others felt anger, shame and confusion, their futures clouded by cycles of despondency and dispair. The long-term erosion of self-identity and self-esteem contributed to high rates of alcoholism and suicides in rural Alaska. Today numerous Native communities are actively involved in sobriety efforts. Some villages prohibit the importation, sale and use of alcohol, with searches of incoming freight and visitors. The efforts also include sobriety camps and healing ceremonies emphasizing Native spirituality.

Politics

One of the landmarks for Alaska Natives came in 1971 with passage of the Alaska Native Claims Settlement Act. It was the climax to many years of political activity by Alaska Natives, and it set the stage for even more.

First, a little background. In 1912, Tlingit and Haida people formed the Alaska Native Brotherhood to win citizenship; at the time, Natives had no rights under the U.S. government. The ANB and its sister organization Alaska Native Sisterhood, still in existence today, were forerunners of later Native organizations including the Tlingit-Haida Central Council and the Alaska Federation of Natives.

In 1935, Congress passed legislation allowing Natives to sue the federal government for land taken by the United States. The Tlingit-Haida council was the first to file a claim for lands taken for Tongass National Forest. In 1958, the Alaska Statehood Act recognized Native rights to some lands and Native land claims continued accumulating. Soon the entire state was tied up in litigation, and in fall 1966 a coalition of Natives formed to push a federal settlement of Native claims through Congress. The new Alaska Federation of Natives found unexpected allies in oil companies, particularly after the North Slope discovery of the Prudhoe Bay field. The AFN claims, supported by the oil companies wanting to settle the issue and proceed with construction of an oil pipeline, resulted in the Alaska Native Claims Settlement Act. It created 13 regional Native corporations and 205 village corporations to manage an endowment of $1 billion and 44 million acres.

The original act made no provisions to extend corporation shares to Native children born after ANCSA's passage, and it allowed non-Natives to eventually buy into the corporations; amendments to change these provisions were later passed. ANCSA corporations were mandated to return profits to their shareholders, which has often been achieved by harvesting timber or extracting minerals, sometimes conflicting with more traditional Native land uses.

An unexpected outcome of ANCSA was that it triggered a resurgence of tribal claims of sovereignty in Alaska, notes Will Mayo, president of Tanana Chiefs Conference Inc., a social services agency for Interior Natives. "The bill was badly written in terms of preserving

and continuing the existence of Native people as an identifiable group," he says. "The corporations exist and many Native people are deeply involved in them and have benefited. So they are a part of who we are. Nevertheless, more and more villages have transferred village corporation lands to tribal governments.... Tribal governments are asserting more rights. The question before the courts is: Do Alaska tribes have powers of other tribes in the nation?"

Tribal status has specific meaning under federal law for Native self-government. This includes giving tribal governments control of such things as adoptions and foster placement of Native children, handling misdemeanor

Kathryn Smith (right), daughter Barbie Smith (center) and cousin Flora Brown cut salmon at Hooper Bay. (Roy Corral)

cases through tribal courts and in some cases levying taxes and managing wildlife on tribal lands. Tribal governments in Alaska have achieved some of these powers, but not all.

At issue is whether tribal powers in Alaska will extend to fish and game management. Subsistence is one of the most heated political issues in Alaska. Currently, Natives have priority for subsistence over commercial and sport uses on federal lands through a "rural

ABOVE: *Lee McCotter, an Athabaskan from Tanana, competes in the one-arm reach during the World Eskimo Indian Olympics, an annual gathering in Fairbanks where athletes from Alaska and other circumpolar nations compete in traditional Native games of skill.* (Patrick J. Endres)

ABOVE RIGHT: *Outfitted in dance regalia, Vanessa Philemonoff takes a break during a performance with* Ataqan Akun, *an Aleut dance group on St. Paul Island.* (Roy Corral)

preference" in the 1981 Alaska National Interest Lands Conservation Act. The courts are deadlocked over the matter of whether this

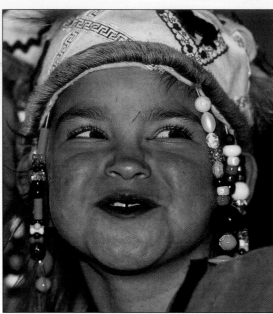

priority extends to state lands. Many Native leaders worry that Congress will someday amend ANILCA to remove this protection. Some of them see tribal powers as a way to maintain Native priorities to fish and game.

Subsistence is "an important part of the larger historical question about the status, rights and future survival of Alaska's aboriginal peoples," according to a 1994 report from the Alaska Natives Commission. "The economies of most Native villages in Alaska remain underdeveloped, artificial dependencies of government where few jobs and relatively small amounts of cash exist. Without a secure protein base of wild, renewable fish and game resources, the poorest and most traditional villagers are doomed to economic and social deterioration.... In addition to supplying food and other necessities, (subsistence) provides

people with productive labor, personal self-esteem, strong family and community relationships, and a cultural foundation that can never be replaced or duplicated by any other arrangement."

United But Separate

Outside the political arena, some of the most visible aspects of Alaska's diverse Native cultures are seen today in expressions of dance and arts.

There is no mistaking Yup'ik dancers with their dance fans and kuspuks for Tlingit dancers in button robes and Chilkat weavings, or for Athabaskans in beaded buckskin regalia. Subtle variations in such items as dance fans, headdresses, and style and trim of robes, kuspuks and parkas identify specific villages, clans or regions within each culture.

Traditional expressions of Native art also vary between many of the cultures. Athabaskans are noted for birchbark baskets, beading and porcupine quill embroidery, and skin sewing. Distinctive to the Aleut culture are finely woven grass baskets. Ivory scrimshaw, baleen basketry, and fur and skin sewing are some of the better known Inupiat arts. The Southeast Indian groups produced master woodworkers, men who carved giant totem poles, house posts and canoes and who were skilled in steaming and bending wood to make boxes of all sizes and descriptions. The women wove spruce root and cedar bark baskets and ceremonial robes from bark, wool and furs. Some Native artists today draw upon their cultural heritage in producing contemporary works, while others focus on more traditional designs and techniques.

Languages are another area where the cultures are different, and even within a single language, numerous dialects may still be heard. But across the cultures, people passed on their histories and rules for living through stories of one form or another. Children were warned against bad behaviors through cautionary tales. Other stories told about relationships between animals and people. The Raven, with dual personalities as creator and trickster, appears as a central character in many stories from different groups.

Although oral narratives are no longer the primary method of information transmission, linguists and Native speakers have done considerable work in documenting languages and stories. Most of this work has been supported or conducted by the Alaska Native Language Center, which opened in 1972 and is the nation's leading research center on Eskimo and Northern Athabaskan languages.

Every culture worldwide celebrates with food, and so it is with Alaska's Native people. This spans everything from the simple act of providing Elders with fresh salmon to the sharing by Inupiat whalers of each bowhead landed, to the ceremonial distribution of a Yup'ik boy's first seal, to potlatches with dancing to celebrate Tlingit totem raisings.

Cultural Revitalization

Many things occurring among Native Alaskans today fall into the category of "cultural revitalization." This includes the recent establishment of cultural centers and museums in places like Bethel, Kodiak and Akutan, and similar efforts in Unalaska and Barrow. These centers serve as repositories for cultural artifacts and offer central meeting places for the communities.

Under a federal repatriation act, many human remains and ceremonial objects taken in archaeological excavations and ethnographic collecting trips earlier this century and housed in museums outside Alaska are now being sent home. In addition, archaeologists handling new excavations today consult with Elders and work closely with Natives in the communities to ensure appropriate cultural handling of the materials.

Culture camps, where Elders share traditional knowledge with youngsters and adults, are increasingly popular as a way for Native people to reconnect with their heritage.

There are also the numerous language and oral history projects in schools and communities. Efforts also are underway throughout Alaska by various organizations to document Native place names and stories that go with them. In addition, dance festivals and other events, such as totem raisings, give Native people opportunities to celebrate their cultures in meaningful ways and revive ceremonies that fell into disuse early this century.

A bold new cooperative effort by the Alaska Federation of Natives, University of Alaska and the National Science Foundation calls for integrating traditional Native knowledge into the state's rural schools. In its infancy in 1995, the Rural Systemic Initiative has among its many goals to strengthen Alaska Native self-identity and to recognize the contributions of Native people, to integrate Native ways of knowing and teaching into the curriculum, and improve Alaska Native students academic performance in science.

Clearly, Native cultures in Alaska have undergone many changes in a relatively short period of time. Yet they are enduring, with the resilience of ever-adapting people. ∎

Hans Alexie keeps in practice for basketball season by shooting hoops at his family's summer fish camp on the Kuskokwim River downstream from Bethel. Basketball is an overwhelmingly popular sport among youngsters and adults in rural Alaska. (Erik Hill, Anchorage Daily News*)*

Aleut

The people known as Aleut, who call themselves *Unangax̂* (oo nung' ah), claim the volcanic, windswept arc of southwest Alaska. Their homelands stretch about 1000 miles through the ocean from the far western tip of the Aleutian Islands to the lower third of the Alaska Peninsula, including the nearby Shumagin Islands and more northerly Pribilof Islands.

Today, of the *Unangax̂* in Alaska, about 2,000 still live in the region's 10 villages — Atka, Nikolski, Akutan, Unalaska, False Pass, Nelson Lagoon, King Cove, Sand Point, St. Paul and St. George. This comprises just over a third of their homeland's total civilian population; several islands once occupied by Aleut people are now military reserves. Almost as many Aleuts live elsewhere in Alaska as in their home territory.

Like many other Alaska Natives today, Aleuts are mobile members of modern society, pursuing jobs, education and other

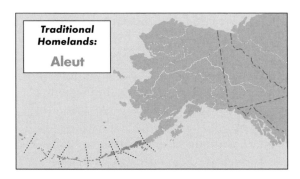

Traditional Homelands:

Aleut

opportunities wherever they lead. Yet cultural practices — fishing, seal hunting, gathering beach foods — remain important, particularly for those who depend on subsistence foods. "You know, we say when the tide is out the table is set," comments Patricia Lekanoff Gregory, 37, of Unalaska. "We're always getting gumboots [chitons] and sea eggs [urchins] for the Elders. You can eat the sea eggs raw, just cut them in half and scoop out the roe." Gumboots are eaten raw or slightly steamed, dipped in butter and garlic. "You

just clink one off the rock, cut off the bony part in back and eat the tongue. They're real chewy, but have a good taste."

In some Aleut communities, particularly those of the Alaska Peninsula, people commercial salmon fish for a living. Several communities host huge fishing ports and international seafood processing plants to serve Bering Sea pollock and cod trawlers. Relatively few Aleuts participate directly in these fisheries, although some village corporations are involved in shore-based fishery developments or share in Bering Sea

FACING PAGE: *Performers from Atka astounded audiences with Aleut dance during the 1996 Arctic Winter Games in Chugiak. Dance has been revived in several Aleut villages after an absence of many decades, a time when "dancing fell asleep." (Erik Hill,* Anchorage Daily News*)*

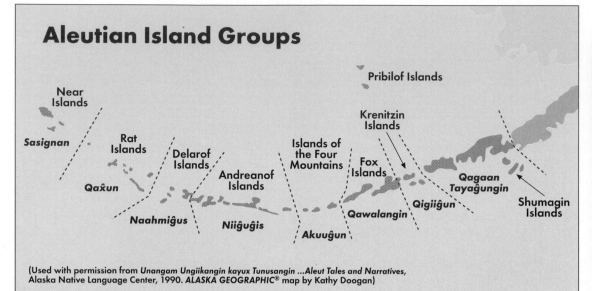

Aleutian Island Groups

Near Islands

Sasignan

Rat Islands

Qax̂un

Delarof Islands

Andreanof Islands

Naahmiĝus

Niiĝuĝis

Akuuĝun

Islands of the Four Mountains

Pribilof Islands

Krenitzin Islands

Fox Islands

Qawalangin

Qigiiĝun

Qagaan Tayaĝungin

Shumagin Islands

(Used with permission from *Unangam Ungiikangin kayux Tunusangin ...Aleut Tales and Narratives,* Alaska Native Language Center, 1990. *ALASKA GEOGRAPHIC®* map by Kathy Doogan)

LEFT: *Peat Galaktionoff gaffs salmon in Sheep Creek at Nikolski. This Umnak Island village has been continuously occupied by Aleuts for 4,000 years. Located on nearby Anangula Island is another ancient site with 8,000-year-old stone tools. (Marion Stirrup)*

ABOVE: *Aquilina Bourdukofsky of St. Paul cleans a seal skin. She works with the Pribilof Stewardship Program that unites young people with Elders to learn cultural traditions; the program also connects traditional Native knowledge with Western scientific methods. (Roy Corral)*

The Ataqan Akun *(We are One) Dance Group performs Aleut songs and dances three times a week in St. Paul. This group and its counterpart on St. George formed in 1992 for youngsters; adults have since formed their own group known as the Seal Island Dancers. (Roy Corral)*

bottom-fish harvests through community development quotas.

Today's waterborne commerce is a modern version of what has been going on in Aleut country for centuries. Early *Unangax̂* traveled and traded extensively in their region and beyond. This watery thoroughfare also brought Aleuts the earliest and harshest contact with outsiders of any of Alaska's Native people.

Russian fur traders sailed into the Aleutian Islands in the mid-1700s to exploit the region's abundance of sea otters. They found an estimated 12,000 to 15,000 indigenous people in seasonal camps and villages, who formed about eight tribes by island groups (see map on facing page). The Russians called them "Aleuts," a Siberian term they also used for the more easterly Alutiiq, coastal people with similar lifestyles but a different language and the traditional enemy of the *Unangax̂*.

The Russians marveled at the Aleuts' seafaring skills in their lightweight, skin-covered kayaks; they knew fur trading success depended on Aleut hunters. Aleut resistance was fierce, but the gun-wielding Russians exerted control and settled. Traders took Aleut men on months-long sea otter hunts as far away as California and Hawaii. The remaining villagers suffered without their

hunters and became more dependent for food and clothing on the Russians. Absence of the Aleut men also disrupted the passing on of ceremonies, dancing and storytelling. The Aleuts were further decimated by infectious disease epidemics. Within a half-century of Russian occupation, only about 2,500 Aleuts remained.

Elements of Russian influence are still evident among Aleut people. Russian surnames today are a legacy of long-ago marriages between traders and Aleut women. Similarly,

the Russian Orthodox religion — introduced with a mission to Alaska in 1841 — still has a devoted following. The saintly priest Ivan Veniaminov, sympathetic to Aleut culture, worked with *Unangam* scholars to develop a written alphabet, taught people to read their language and conducted services in it.

Today, the *Unangam* language is spoken by Elders and middle-aged adults, used in special church services and taught in schools. In Atka, one of the most traditional Aleut villages, children still speak the language at home.

Two dialects of Aleut remain — Western Aleut, spoken on Atka, and Eastern Aleut, spoken elsewhere. A renewed interest in language and storytelling, a revival of Aleut dance and efforts by communities such as Unalaska and Akutan to establish cultural centers and museums reflect an increasing interest in the heritage of the *Unangax̂*.

The early Aleuts were masters of their treeless, maritime environment, using driftwood, rocks, grasses, fish skins, animal bones and bird feathers for tools, shelter and clothing. The women painstakingly wove grass for many uses — sleeping mats, socks and vessels tight enough to hold water. Aleut baskets woven today command premium prices. Aleut men were renowned for their boat-making skills, their signature craft being the *iqyax̂*, skin-covered kayaklike craft. Today, the art of *iqyax̂*-building has re-emerged as a cultural connection. High school students in Unalaska recently completed two of these boats: one, a wide-bodied *iqyax̂* for fishing or carrying cargo; the other of classic split-bow design, built narrow and long for speed. After practicing in the high school's Olympic-sized pool, they paddle in the village lake and Unalaska Bay. The Aleut youngsters displayed almost immediate proficiency with the boats, said Gregory, almost as if they were born to it.

Today, Russian Orthodox churches throughout the region are being restored, partly with federal funds received in 1989, as a belated settlement for the Aleuts' treatment during World War II. The war brought Allied military occupation, Japanese invasion, and nearly a year of air, sea and ground combat. Attu villagers were captured by the enemy; the U.S. government shipped most other Aleuts to desolate internment camps in Southeast where one of every 10 people died.

FACING PAGE: *Larry Merculief, an Aleut from St. Paul and general manager of the Central Bering Sea Fishermen's Association, is active in issues concerning the Bering Sea ecosystem, fishing and Natives. Below him, northern fur seals congregate on shore with St. Paul village in the distance. The Russians moved Aleuts to the Pribilof Islands in 1786 to live and harvest fur seals. After U.S. purchase of Alaska, the islanders continued harvesting seals for the government until commercial slaughter was outlawed in 1983. Today, large fishing ports and tourism fuel the economy. (Roy Corral)*

RIGHT: *Moses Gordieff (right) and a friend pick fish from their setnet in Unalaska, in view of shipping activity at the Port of Dutch Harbor. Aleut villagers value subsistence activities and want to prevent water pollution from fuel residues and wastes off passing ships. (Karen Jettmar)*

Reparation funds are being used in a massive restoration of the 100-year-old Church of the Holy Ascension of Christ in Unalaska, once considered one of the nation's 12 most endangered historic landmarks. ■

LEFT: *Vladimir Melovidov of St. Paul picks wild celery, a food basic to the Aleut diet for centuries and still enjoyed today. (Roy Corral)*

BELOW: *Titiana Zaochney, of Atka, learned the intricate art of grass basketry from her godmother, Annie Golley, in the 1950s. She gathers beach grass each summer and splits each blade into 8 to 10 strands, some finer than thread. She enjoys the challenge of weaving. "It takes patience and hours to do so," she says. (Harry M. Walker)*

Riding Ungiikan *Home*

By Barbara Švarný Carlson

Editor's note: *Barbara Švarný Carlson lives in Anchorage with her husband and two sons where she continues researching and telling Ungiikan. Formerly an elementary school teacher, she is now writing a teacher's guide to selected stories from ...Aleut Tales and Narratives. She has been inspired by Unangan artists in her family, including her mother Gertrude Švarný, well-known for her basketry and sculptures of ivory, bone, baleen and stone, as well as oils and watercolors.*

Thomas Wolfe said, "You can't go home again." Having lived for many years away from my "village" of Unalaska in the Aleutian Islands, I find that a disturbing thought. For me, the *Ungiikan*, the old stories of the *Unangax̂*, Aleutian Aleuts, are the ticket for a metaphorical return trip. As I study and learn more about the stories, I learn more about what it means to be *Unangax̂*.

Growing up in Unalaska in the 1950s and '60s with three younger sisters, I learned as much as anyone was learning at the time about our culture. We were raised rich with relatives who lived nearby or visited often. Our mother, Gertrude Hope Švarný — of *Unangax̂*, English, and possibly Russian heritage — had lived most of her life in Unalaska. Our father, Samuel Švarný of Slovakian heritage, had been in Unalaska for years. They spent time taking us special places outdoors, teaching us many uses for Native foods. We developed an appreciation for *udax̂* (dry fish), *chadux̂* (seal oil), *lustux̂* (pickled sea lion flipper) and *qungaayux̂* (the hump from a humpback salmon). We learned to never harvest more than we could use or share.

There were things, however, that we did not learn, such as the old stories, our language, and the name by which our ancestors had called themselves. We did not know that we were *Unangax̂* nor that we were of the *Qawalangin* Tribe of Unalaska. The name "Aleut" was used by the Russians as they moved from *Atux̂* (Attu Island) eastward through Alaska during the 18th century. The term "Aleut" was eventually adopted by our people, contributing to the erosion of our indigenous culture.

Though proud to be Aleut, I began to realize that many other Alaska Native people appeared to know more about their heritage. In the 1970s, I was privileged to assist with the Alaska Native Heritage Festival at the Anchorage Museum of History and Art. The dynamic Native orators at this

Barbara Švarný Carlson visits in Unalaska with Nick Galaktionoff, an Unangax̂ Elder who helps her learn Ungiikan. He and Barbara's father, Sam Švarný, fished together from rocking chairs in a small boat, where they'd sit and talk for hours waiting for halibut to bite. Today, Galaktionoff shares stories and knowledge of the old ways learned from his Elders. (Samuel Švarný)

LEFT: *Barbara Švarný Carlson helped name this orphaned sea otter Chuluugl, Unangam for "young seagull," during its rehabilitation at the Bird Treatment Center in Anchorage. (Stuart Beard, courtesy of Barbara Carlson)*

ABOVE: *Barbara Švarný Carlson tells* Ungiikan *during the Ounalashka Corp. banquet in Unalaska. Her traditional bentwood hunting visor and drum were made by her mother, Gertrude Švarný. (Gertrude Švarný, courtesy of Barbara Carlson)*

festival often gave their names of self-designation — Inupiat instead of Eskimo, Tsimshian instead of Indian. I wondered if we Aleuts had ever called ourselves something else. Mom said she had learned we were *Unangax̂*. This sent me searching to learn more.

Storytelling emerged as an important link to my *Unangax̂* culture when I became a parent. My children needed to know about their heritage. They needed

to hear the old stories, the *Ungiikan*. They needed to see people living the culture, dancing

and telling stories, to have these things to teach their children. But I had been told for years that our language was gone and that hardly anyone had heard the old stories. Then I received *Stories Out of Slumber* (1979), a book of *Ungiikan* rewritten by Unalaska teacher Ray Hudson. His sensitivity helped me brave the ethnocentric bias present in much of the literature, to sift through misinformation and try to find the truth.

While grateful that information was available, I also felt embarrassed and disconcerted to have to depend on writings by our conquerors and other non-*Unangax̂*. Why could I not learn these things from my own people? The *Unangax̂* had survived by integrating with the dominant cultures, first Russian, then American. Many traditional ways, including telling the old stories, fell into disuse as our people mastered new cultural and language skills. But despite this, not all was forgotten. Some Elders have courageously decided to discuss the old ways.

The work of scholars helps me know what questions to ask. What grounds my work, however, is to ask the tradition-keepers whether certain things are true or not. It would be easier if I spoke *Unangam Tunuu*. My eldest son

and I studied for a semester with *Unangax̂* linguist Moses Dirks at Alaska Pacific University, but fluency would require much more time and work. Consequently, rather than learning stories from the Elders, I rely on the definitive *Unangam Ungiikangin Kayux Tunusangin... Aleut Tales and Narratives*, collected in 1909-1910 by Waldemar Jochelson and edited by Knut Bergsland and Dirks (1990). Next, I try to find clues from words and phrases in the language and anthropological texts to discern the context in which a story was originally told. Finally, I take what I have learned back to "the village" and ask questions.

Nick Galaktionoff, an old friend of my father's from Unalaska, has been especially helpful. On more than one occasion, my dad told him to talk to me because I studied the old stories. As our friendship grew, Nick and I began to work together informally as master and apprentice.

The *Unangax̂* way of life was taught and perpetuated through oral tradition, in which important information was committed to memory and passed on by countless generations through stories. This oral tradition includes: *Ungiikan*, or stories from a time long ago when things were very different; *Kadaangaadan*, narrative stories from more recent times that frequently include names of actual people and places; and *Tunusan*, accounts of life exactly as it happened or could have happened. This oral tradition formed the framework of our *Unangax̂* education system.

Oral tradition is a different way of learning, because it depends on memory. I was driven to learn new and difficult things to train my mind, such as doing crossword puzzles, decoding cryptograms and learning to read music to play piano. Nick was educated in the traditional *Unangax̂* way among Elders, and he has an exceptional memory. He was incredulous when, as we began to discuss something he had told me, I scurried back to check my notes. Try as I may, my brain seems too rigid to function by memory alone. I need my books, paper and computers. Nick needs only his natural faculties.

In traditional *Unangax̂* education, a person might hear a story 50 times during his or her lifetime, learning a little more each time about the right way to live. Likewise good storytellers could read their audiences and know what people might need to hear

or have emphasized.

The integrity of this oral tradition was protected by protocol. One rule was to know all of a story — beginning, middle, and ending — before telling it. When storytellers achieved mastery, and only then, they stepped into the role of teacher. To do otherwise could corrupt the lessons that were the intent of the stories.

Today, we are at a critical time in our culture: There are Elders still alive who know some of these stories and can discuss their meanings. If I tell the stories now, even though I am still learning, they can give me advice and my children can hear the stories as children. Fortunately, more people are telling the stories now than a few years ago.

Through *Ungiikan*, we learn that some of the same ethics we now value, the traditional *Unangax̂* valued; that some of the same things we consider sacred, the traditional *Unangax̂* considered sacred; that some of what we fear was also feared by the traditional *Unangax̂*.

One can be *Unangax̂* anywhere, but people in the villages are living closest to the heart of tradition. Not only do they live on the land of our ancestors, under the same skies, using the

same resources, but their daily activities carry the memories of those who lived before. I have often seen people of my mother's generation lament that they wish they knew more, then proceed to share precious memories. Eyes light up, someone else enters the conversation, and people begin to mentally revitalize their pasts as they collaborate. Some of what is true about our people remains embedded in the culture today, almost too close to be seen by those closest to it.

As I walk around a lake near where I live in the big city, I watch the colors change through the year and the ways ice crystals form around rocks in creeks before the water freezes over; but I think about *Unangax̂* in the villages. I think about words, phrases, and concepts from *Ungiikan* such as knowing we call the sun's afterglow *x̂aniĝilix̂*; that we know Orion's Belt as "Three Large Men Looking Down;" that we share a precious closeness with our lands, skies and waters; and that *Tutada*, the instruction to "listen," is a crucial lifelong lesson. I envision the plants, rocks and animals of those places, and arrange my landscape here to resemble Unalaska as I think about our stories. It takes me home. □

The Song Sparrow

Song Sparrow and his cousin Wren set out beachcombing. They walked on until they found a whale. Upon reaching the whale, Wren entered its blowhole and began to eat inside there. After eating he came out and went back home together with his cousin.

The next morning he again started out to that whale with his cousin. Reaching the whale, he again entered its blowhole and began to eat there. After eating he tried in vain to get out of there. Upon trying in vain to get out, he said to his cousin, "Pull my leg!" whereupon his cousin went over to him and, pulling him by his leg, pulled his leg off.

Having pulled his leg off, he said to him, "Did I kill you?"

Wren said, "No, today is not the occasion for dying."

When [Wren] had him pull on one of his wings in turn, it was also pulled off. When the other one was in its turn pulled off, he prepared to have him pull him by his head. His cousin Song Sparrow pulled him by his head until he pulled off his head in its turn. Having pulled his head off, he said, "Hey in there, did I kill you?" [Wren] did not make a sound, however, so Song Sparrow had lost his cousin and returned.

That fellow Wren had been eating inside the whale until he got too fat to be able to get out and died, so the story goes.

— One example of *Ungiikan*, dictated by Arseniy Kryukov, Umnak, January 1910. Reprinted from ...*Aleut Tales and Narratives* (1990) with permission from Moses Dirks, ed., and the Alaska Native Language Center.

Alutiiq

In the village of Akhiok on Kodiak Island during a recent "Alutiiq Days" cultural celebration, people gathered around Elder Larry Matfay. He positioned an arrow across the bow as he explained the game of *howaq*. This bow-and-arrow game tested hunters' skill at piercing kelp bulbs; the bulbs presented a target similar to that of a sea otter head bobbing in the water. Matfay remembers playing *howaq* as a child, but the game died out when villagers stopped hunting sea otters early in this century. But *howaq* was about to make a comeback. It is one of numerous pieces of Alutiiq culture that Matfay now shares with people anxious to learn more about their traditions.

Similar reawakenings are going on throughout Alaska's Alutiiq region. For instance, in Kodiak the Alutiiq Museum opened as a cultural and research center and artifact depository; it is one of few Native-owned and operated museums in the nation. Another example is the *Nuuciq* spirit camp on Nuchek

Island in Prince William Sound. This cultural retreat brings Elders and youth together at the site of an ancient Alutiiq village and important trading center; Fort Konstantine, built in 1793, was the main Russian post for the sound.

Spirit camp activities include everything from blazing trails and story-telling to filleting salmon and braiding seal gut. Perhaps as much as anything, spirit camps give people a reprieve from the demands of modern life, allowing them to reconnect with the basics of personal, community and cultural survival. "I learned old beliefs and stories that had meaning to them," said Elmer Moonin, 18, from Port Graham who attended the camp in 1995. "If you think about it and try to imagine how these people lived not too long ago in the place where we were, it's amazing. Some of the old beliefs and stories are still told and passed on generation to generation."

"We're going to have a *Nuuciq* flag-raising party in 1996," asserts camp organizer John F.C. Johnson. He notes that the Spanish claimed Nuchek territory with a Christian cross and service; the English claimed it with a bottle of coins; the Russians put up their flag and

FACING PAGE: *The Alutiiq Museum (blue-roofed building, center right) in downtown Kodiak opened in spring 1995 as an exhibit gallery and cultural center emphasizing Alutiiq heritage. (Marion Stirrup)*

FAR LEFT: *Dr. Lora Johnson, an Alutiiq now doing archaeological work in her ancestral homeland of Prince William Sound, found these artifacts — a stone lamp, adze and grinding stones — at a prehistoric site on Nuchek Island. (John F. C. Johnson)*

LEFT: *Larry Matfay, 89, grew up in Akhiok where he was educated in traditional Alutiiq style by village Elders who taught him to hunt, trap, track game, preserve furs, catch and smoke fish and read the weather, among other things. Formerly a fisherman and bear guide, Matfay spends many hours these days with school children, telling stories, teaching tool-making and boat-building, and encouraging traditional song and dance. Here he shows students how to use bear intestine, which he has inflated and dried. (Joe Kelley)*

buried a bronze plate bearing a double-headed eagle; and the Americans raised their flag. "The Chugach (Alutiiq) have occupied this area about 4,000 years," says Johnson. "Now we've got a flag we'll put up! It'll be a good windsock for our airstrip."

Special cultural celebrations and spirit camps aside, the Alutiiq people today, particularly those still living in the coastal villages, share in the rich seafaring heritage of their ancestors.

Ancient village sites dating back 7,000 years on Kodiak Island and the Alaska Peninsula reveal that Alutiiq ancestors were accomplished maritime hunters and fishermen. They plied the depths for cod and halibut. They paddled with darts and harpoons after sea lions, seals, sea otters and whales. They took seabirds, such as puffins, and climbed cliffs to gather gull eggs. Seal meat and oil fed them, the oil also fueled their lamps; they used driftwood, sod, thatch, bones, skins and feathers to make their homes, tools, boats and clothing.

Many Alutiiq villagers today remain closely attached to the sea, fishing and living along Alaska's southcentral and southwestern coasts. Seal oil is still a basic food, used as a dressing or dip for dried fish or roe on kelp, or to mix with berries. In some Alutiiq villages, land mammals such as bear and caribou are important in the subsistence cycle.

The Alutiiq made ingenious adaptations to their environments. Today that is still the case. Fishermen equip their boats with the latest in affordable gadgetry, from electronic depth finders to water-cooled holds to keep their catch fresh. The villages are modernized with frame homes, electricity, grocery stores, computers, satellite television, four-wheelers and daily airplane connections to larger towns.

The early Alutiiq also adopted elements of Aleut, Yup'ik and Tlingit cultures: Those from Prince William Sound used adzed planks and logs along with sod to construct large buildings, hinting at Tlingit plank construction. The more common early Alutiiq dwellings were semi-subterranean sod houses reinforced by whale bones or driftwood, also found in Aleut and Yup'ik country. A spruce root basket recovered from an ancient Kodiak Island site shows environmental adaptations similar to the Tlingit, who also wove spruce roots. Like the Aleut and Yup'ik, the Alutiiq depended on skin-covered kayaks and the larger open skin-boats called *angyaqs.*

Alutiiq territory covers the upper Alaska Peninsula from Port Moller to Egegik on the north and from Kupreanoff Point to Kamishak Bay on the south; it includes Kodiak Island,

parts of lower Cook Inlet and Prince William Sound. Alutiiq villages today include Old Harbor, Akhiok, Karluk, Port Lions, Larsen Bay and Ouzinkie on Kodiak Island, and Tatitlek and Chenega Bay in Prince William Sound; Cordova hosts one of the largest groups of Alutiiq in the sound. Natives of Alutiiq descent also live in Alaska Peninsula villages such as Chignik and Port Heiden. People throughout the region, however, often describe themselves to outsiders as Aleut. The Russians applied the name "Aleut" liberally when identifying the Natives they encountered, although they further designated the Kodiak Islanders as Koniag and those in Prince

William Sound as Chugach. The Alutiiq language, *Sugcestun*, is part of the Aleut-Eskimo linguistic family and is closely related to Yup'ik. About 450 of the estimated 3,000 Alutiiq people still speak some of the language today; less than 200 are fluent speakers. The Alutiiq term of self-designation in *Sugcestun* is *Sugpiaq*, which means "genuine" or "real person."

The question of Alutiiq identity, as examined by Gordon Pullar on page 31, is

RIGHT: *Susan Malutin, an accomplished Alutiiq skin sewer in Kodiak, stitches a bearded seal gut kamleika, a traditional waterproof parka worn by hunters. Malutin said her husband, Roger, who was born on Afognak Island, plans to wear the kamleika when it's finished. To learn to sew waterproof seams, a technique that incorporates beach grass, Malutin apprenticed under Grace Harrod, who lives in Kodiak and learned skin sewing from her mother Mary Smith, of Nunivak Island. (Marion Stirrup)*

FAR RIGHT: *Phillip McCormick paddles an Alutiiq-style baidarka made in Kodiak as part of a promotion for a baidarka conference. His Alutiiq ancestors in the 1700s would have presented a similar image as they headed out to hunt sea mammals, such as sea lions, whales or sea otters. McCormick wears a replica bentwood hunting hat and prepares to launch his dart from a throwing board, which extended the hunter's striking range. (Marion Stirrup)*

ABOVE: *Madelyn Brown performs with the Shoon'aq Tribal Dancers, who formed in 1983 to help revive Alutiiq tradition. (Danny Daniels)*

ABOVE RIGHT: *Students at Nanwalek, an Alutiiq community on the lower Kenai Peninsula, hold traditional baidarkas they are making with the help of community volunteers. (Fred Deussing)*

of growing importance to the people as they define their culture in context of contemporary society. Pullar and other Alutiiq leaders are

planning an Alutiiq conference to talk about this issue among others; the conference may be held along with an exhibit of Alutiiq artifacts taken from Alaska in the late 1800s, now held by the Smithsonian Institution. Curated by Aron Crowell of the Smithsonian's Arctic Studies Center in Anchorage, the ambitious undertaking includes an interactive exhibit so visitors can hear Alutiiq people talking about modern food gathering and fishing or Elders talking about how items were made and used, as well as telling stories in their own language. Students in Tatitlek are helping develop the exhibit by interviewing Elders in their village for histories, information and stories.

In researching this exhibit, Crowell also videotaped four master skin sewers from the Alutiiq, Inupiat and Yup'ik regions discussing a 100-year-old squirrel skin parka at the Smithsonian. The women said the maker had used her raw materials fully — the noses of the squirrels remained on the pelts — and had taken extreme care in sewing. The parka showed Alutiiq and Yup'ik designs. "It was an everyday hunting parka but it was equally as beautiful as a festive parka," recalls Kodiak skin sewer Susan Malutin. She plans to make a replica using about 60 squirrel pelts. "To think that someone that far back took that much time in far more primitive conditions.... There was such a culture here, and on an everyday basis they wore these things." ■

Indigenous Identity on Kodiak Island

By Gordon L. Pullar

Editor's note: *Gordon L. Pullar, a Kodiak Island Alutiiq currently living in Anchorage, is director of the Alaska Native Human Resource Development Program, College of Rural Alaska, University of Alaska. He has been involved in tribal self-determination and cultural revitalization efforts for the past two decades, including serving six years as president of the Kodiak Area Native Association. He currently chairs the steering committee for the Arctic Studies Center of the Smithsonian Institution and sits on the boards of the Koniag Educational Foundation and Keepers of the Treasures, a national organization formed to address issues related to the protection of indigenous cultures. He is pursuing his doctoral degree in Organizational Anthropology and International Studies through the Union Institute in Cincinnati, Ohio.*

The angry reaction was swift, just as I had feared. The Native woman in the audience loudly objected at the first mention of the word "Eskimo."

It was 1985, and anthro-pologist Dick Jordan was giving a presentation in Kodiak about an archaeological project on the island. This was his second summer working on the project, and he was confused and distressed by the Native peoples' insistence that they were Aleuts. Their language, after all, was Eskimoan, very close to Yup'ik. He said he would diplomatically explain to the Native people in the audience that they were Eskimos, not Aleuts.

Most people had heard this before and resented it. In their lifetimes they had always been "Aleuts," or in their own language Alutiiqs. Some of the elders remembered referring to them-selves as *Sugpiaq*, meaning "a real person," but few used that term anymore. Of one thing they were certain: They were not Eskimos.

Kodiak's Native people have gone through a number of changes since first contact with Russians in 1763, and events and conditions since that time have profoundly impacted who people feel they are.

After nearly 8,000 years of cultural survival, the indigenous people of Kodiak Island came under the rule of outside forces when the first permanent Russian settlement was established there in 1784. Since then, the culture and identity of the people have been under pressure. On Aug. 13, 1784, Russian merchant Gregorii Shelikhov, with two ships

Throughout Alutiiq territory, the onion-shaped domes of Russian Orthodox churches speak to the long-lasting influence of Russian contact. The Orthodox faith has many devout practitioners in Native Alaska, evidenced in part by the care given to their chapels, such as this one — Ascension of Our Lord — at Karluk on Kodiak Island (Don Pitcher)

Students from Old Harbor learn the traditional practice of spearing salmon for food. (Joe Kelley)

armed with cannons, launched a decisive attack against the people of Kodiak Island. Casualties were severe. As many as 2,000 Alutiiqs sought protection on a refuge rock, a small island with cliffs that dropped sharply to the sea. Many hundreds perished, as the Russians shelled the small island with cannon fire and then stormed it with armed men.

This was the first in a series of events that traumatized the Alutiiq people and confused their identity.

These included severe disease epidemics such as the smallpox epidemic of 1837 to 1840, which killed so many people that Russian administrators consolidated Kodiak Island's 65 villages into only seven. Others were natural disasters which destroyed villages and forced survivors to relocate. These included the devastating eruption of Mt. Katmai in 1912 that destroyed villages on the Alaska Peninsula, and the great

earthquake and tsunami of 1964, which destroyed villages on Kodiak Island and in Prince William Sound.

Last summer, my 10-year-old son, Gordon Jr., and I visited friends in the Kodiak Island village of Old Harbor. Although born in Kodiak, my son has lived in Anchorage since he was 5 and therefore has perhaps developed a different sense of identity than he might have developed had he still resided in Kodiak. He was excited about the visit to a Kodiak village and was anxious to meet other "Aleut" children. He quickly made friends with a boy his age and asked him, "Are you an Aleut?" "No, I'm not an Aleut," the boy quickly responded somewhat indignantly. "I'm a Native!"

This interchange is symbolic, in a way, of the issue of identity on Kodiak Island. In another village a few years ago, a woman who had lived in the village her entire life asked me in frustration, "Who are we anyway? Are we Aleuts, Alutiiqs or Eskimos?" She

said she felt embarrassed that anthropologists were claiming that we were Eskimos and seemingly had proof to support their claim.

Russian occupation on Kodiak Island (1784 to 1867) significantly influenced the way the island's Native people see themselves. Clothing, foods, language, surnames and, most importantly, the Russian Orthodox religion are the most noticeable.

As the American period progressed, Native people realized they were not looked on as equals and many tried to find ways to obscure their Native heritage. One way on Kodiak, where many had Russian surnames, was to emphasize their Russian backgrounds.

Making matters worse was existence of a social class called "Creoles," which had been created by the Russians. One way to be Creole was to have mixed Russian-Native parentage. Another was to be educated in Russian ways and be promoted as an overseer for the Russian fur traders. This Creole designation was used on birth certificates well into the 20th century.

My late uncle Karl Armstrong Jr. said people were taught that Creoles were "half as good as a Russian and twice as good as a

Native." Therefore it was desirable to identify as a Russian if possible. My mother Olga Vasilie Rossing, for example, would identify herself first as a Russian and secondly as a Native. She was born in 1916 to Vasili Rossing and Afanasiia Rysev. Her father, however, had been born as Vasili Shmakov in 1885; he adopted the name Rossing from his stepfather.

At one of the archaeological presentations of the 1980s mentioned earlier, a woman from one of the villages gazed with tears in her eyes at the well-preserved carved wooden ceremonial masks, woven spruce root baskets and other tools. She said, almost to herself, "I guess we really are Natives after all. I was always told that we were Russians."

These identifications came back to haunt people when the Alaska Native Claims Settlement Act (ANCSA) was passed in 1971, and anyone with one-quarter or more Native blood was eligible to enroll. Many of those emphasizing Russian heritage, who had "passed" for non-Natives to gain social and economic acceptance within the dominant society, now enrolled as Natives as they were legally entitled to do. This caused a backlash among other Natives that, to some degree, remains today. One way to insult someone is to say, "He (she) was never a Native until 1971."

The passage of ANCSA produced yet another identity of "shareholder." The regional corporation established under the act for the Kodiak area is called Koniag Inc., and the term "Koniag shareholder" is one of the contemporary descriptive terms for Native people from this area. Even the name chosen for the corporation is reflective of confused identity. The word "Koniag" seemed not ever to have been used in self-description. It apparently derived from *Kanaagin*, the name applied to the people of Kodiak Island by their traditional enemies, the *Unangan* of the Aleutian Islands. The *Sugpiaq*, incidentally, called the *Unangan Taya'ut*.

So how did people come to call themselves Aleut? The term apparently originated in Siberia as "Aliutor," a name applied to a coastal indigenous group on the Kamchatka Peninsula. Russian explorers thought the people they encountered in Alaska were the same, since their ways of life appeared similar, and applied this name first to the *Unangan* and then to the *Sugpiaq*. Like the descriptive terms "Indian" and "Eskimo" also applied by misunderstanding outsiders, Aleut stuck.

Further confusing the names and identity issue is the practice used from the *Sugpiaq* area of naming people as inhabitants of a certain place. This is done by adding the suffix "miut" meaning "people of" to a place name. Examples are *Qikertarmiut*, which refers to all people residing on Kodiak Island and means "people of the island," or *Sun'aqmiut* meaning "people of Kodiak," or *Nuniaqmiut*, "people of Old Harbor."

Today, the people of Kodiak Island are continuing with a revival of a pride in heritage that involves deciding which name to use to describe themselves. While most still say "Aleut" or "Alutiiq" some are in favor of resurrecting the name "Sugpiaq."

The late Nina Olsen, who grew up in the village of Afognak in the 1920s, told me, "When I was growing up in Afognak, I don't remember that we used the terms 'Aleut' or 'Alutiiq' to describe ourselves. We said 'Sugpiaq, a real person.' I think we should go back to calling ourselves *Sugpiaq*. It has so much more meaning."

Whatever name is ultimately decided on, it will be decided by the people themselves and not by others. □

Gordon Pullar and son Gordon Jr., 10, live in Anchorage, but trace their Alutiiq heritage to Kodiak Island. (L.J. Campbell, staff)

Yup'ik

Every March, hundreds of people arrive for Camai Dance Festival in Bethel, a Yup'ik regional hub near the mouth of the Kuskokwim River. They come from villages throughout the region, toting fancy parkas and headdresses trimmed in wolf and wolverine fur, dance fans ruffed with tufts of caribou hair, seal-gut drums, and maybe a few newly carved wooden masks. Most come by airplane and snow machine, but at least a few hook up their dog teams for brisk journeys across the delta's frozen rivers and sloughs. At night, the sounds of howling sled dogs echo through town, an ethereal chorus to the beating of dance drums and Yup'ik words raised in song.

Gatherings such as this occur in towns and villages throughout Alaska's Yup'ik region, often in wintertime when people are generally less busy with fishing, hunting and gathering activities and have only jobs and school to plan around. Community potlatches and dance festivals bring people together, providing

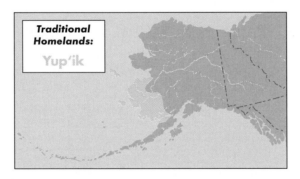

Traditional Homelands:

Yup'ik

important cultural links spanning generations.

Of all of Alaska's Native people, the Yup'ik are the most populous, with a booming birth rate, and have the largest number of individuals who still speak the language. About 20,000 Yup'ik people live in Alaska today, most in small villages along the Bering Sea coast and the lower Yukon and Kuskokwim rivers. Outside the regional centers of Bethel (population 4,600) and Dillingham (population 2,000), Hooper Bay is the largest Yup'ik village — and one of the fastest growing villages in Alaska —

with about 900 people. Most Yup'ik villages are considerably smaller and tend to be made up of extended, interconnected families.

The Yup'ik traditional homelands extend south from Unalakleet River through the fan-shaped deltas of the Yukon and Kuskokwim rivers and down along Bristol Bay, where Yup'ik culture eventually mingles with the Alutiiq and Aleut. In the Yup'ik stronghold of the Yukon and Kuskokwim deltas, many children still grow up speaking Yup'ik at home. In perhaps 17 of the 60 Yup'ik villages, children learn Central Yup'ik as their first language. This is the most widely spoken Yup'ik language with about 10,500 Native speakers. Local radio stations broadcast in the language, school children read Yup'ik texts, and in some places

FACING PAGE: *Yup'ik women cut salmon to hang on drying racks at Hooper Bay. (Roy Corral)*

Villagers celebrate Russian Christmas at St. Seraphim Chapel in Lower Kalskag. The three days of services held in January were led by Father Peter Askoar, a traveling Russian Orthodox priest out of Russian Mission. (Roy Corral)

machines or vehicles, mostly taxis, in winter.

Although some people in most villages work for the state or village government, schools or local stores, cash jobs are generally scarce. Commercial salmon and herring fisheries give many villagers their only opportunities to earn money, so fishing, hunting and gathering remain an integral part of life. While the subsistence harvest of fish, game, birds, greens and berries is an economic and nutritional necessity, it is also much more: It is a lifestyle central to the Yup'ik culture. Connected to the acts of harvesting and gathering are traditional celebrations and stories, through which the people learn how to live and relate to the world around them.

The Yup'ik live close in many respects to the ways of their ancestors and, at the same time, retain their cultural identity in the context of the larger society. For instance, students from the Yupiit School District near Bethel have a presence on the Internet. Janice George, an 8th grader from Akiachak, incorporates sound in her description of village life so that Internet users hear her language, such as her Yup'ik name *Mikiicaq Aqvung'aq.* Here are some of the other things she has to tell people: "In Akiachak there are not highways, no running water except in the teacher's houses and the laundry. People think we live in igloos,

elders can still converse in Yup'ik with their grandchildren. There are numerous dialects of Central Yup'ik, and although subtle variations exist between villages, sometimes giving slightly different meanings to the same word, most of the dialects are mutually intelligible.

Just as their ancestors were hunter-gatherers, so are the modern Yup'ik people. Seasonal activities vary somewhat depending on location, but may include hunting sea mammals such as seal, walrus, and whales; river fishing in summer for salmon and trout, in winter for whitefish and tomcod; gathering wild vegetables, berries and eggs; going into the

uplands and mountains for ground squirrels, moose and caribou; and harvesting ducks, geese and other waterfowl that migrate by the millions each year into the Central Yup'ik region's rich wetlands, part of the Yukon Delta National Wildlife Refuge.

Still, Alaska's Yup'ik villages are hundreds of miles away from paved highways and urban centers, and while they are connected to the outside world by telephones, computers and daily airplane flights, they remain largely self-contained bastions of Yup'ik culture. The region's many waterways are the Yup'ik road system, traveled by boats in summer and snow but we stay in regular houses....In fish camps we don't have any electricity. We have steambath houses where we wash. We cut fish all summer from May to August....We go swimming to my grandma's fish camp or to the sandbars...." And then she includes computerized pictures of her village, her classmates, and a king salmon at fish camp.

Of all of Alaska's Native groups, the Yup'ik were among the last to experience prolonged contact with outsiders and were generally spared foreign intrusion until the early to mid-1800s. The Russians made limited explorations of Yup'ik country, with small expeditions along the Bering Sea coast and occasional forays upriver toward the Interior. The Russian Orthodox Church established a small mission and a few Russian trading posts were opened, including one in Norton Sound at St. Michael. This brought direct access to trade goods, and created a collector's market for Yup'ik-made items such as coiled grass baskets. But, for the most part, the Yup'iks were left alone until after the transfer of Alaska to the United States in 1867.

In the mid-1880s, salmon canneries opened on Bristol Bay and Moravian missionaries arrived on the Kuskokwim River, where they established a church and school across from the Yup'ik village of *Mumtrekhlogamiut*; they called the new settlement "Bethel." The Catholics took the mouth of the Yukon River and later

opened a mission at St. Marys. As in many other parts of Alaska, the early missionaries showed little understanding of aboriginal belief systems and stifled many Yup'ik practices, which included making spirit masks to seek bountiful harvests and holding potlatch feasts and dance celebrations to honor the spirits of people and animals.

Generally, however, the inner delta had few resources to attract explorers and even during the early 20th century, when gold discoveries brought droves of newcomers to parts of

western Alaska, most of the Yup'ik territory was basically ignored except for river corridors. It wasn't until the Alaska Native Claims Settlement Act (1971) and oil development on the North Slope (1970s) that the Yup'ik villages fully felt the grip of modern society. The land claims settlement, combined with the state's windfall of oil revenues, brought rapid change — modern housing, electricity, telephones, daily air service to regional centers, and in some cases, running water and sewage systems.

In recent years, several major religious

Artist Rachel Smart displays some of her basketry and Yup'ik Eskimo dolls at her home in Hooper Bay. (Roy Corral)

denominations have apologized for denouncing the Alaska's Native ways as pagan, and the Yup'ik have embraced their cultural dances and feasting with unbridled enthusiasm. In 1964, when Father Rene Astruc arrived as administrator of the St. Marys mission, he sent out word that he had no objection to potlatches. Within a year, the first was held. Now potlatches and dance festivals draw villages together regularly, occurring almost as often as, and sometime simultaneously with, community basketball tournaments. "People realized you must have dancing," said Andrew Kelly of Emmonak several years ago. "Sometimes we have dancing every night. The dancing spirit is alive. It's very much alive today."

Here's how Torin Kuiggpak Jacobs, of Bethel, describes Eskimo dancing, lamenting how much he misses it during the school year when he attends Loyola University in Chicago: "I take so much pride in dancing to songs that my grandparents have danced and sang, and their grandparents and their grandparents before them. Not only is it the pride, but the

BELOW LEFT: *Nels Hedlund, a Yup'ik sled builder, mushed the mail between Bethel and Aniak during the early 1930s. He and his wife Rose, an Athabaskan from Nondalton, raised their family at a homestead on Lake Iliamna, where he continued making sleds until his death in 1991. He was 77 when this picture was made, a year before he died. (Roz Goodman)*

BELOW: *Jim Hurley of Ekwok, a Yup'ik village on the Nushagak River, inspects subsistence fishing nets. The former mayor of Ekwok, Hurley also fishes commercially in Bristol Bay and trains sled dogs. (Greg Syverson)*

ABOVE: *John Ivanoff, 21, uses spruce boughs to protect moose and bear meat during a September hunting trip. Ivanoff's older cousin Fritz George led about a half-dozen male relatives on the outing from Akiachak, a two-day journey up the Kuskokwim River to Stony River, where they camped and hunted for more than a week. They took two bull moose, a black bear and a brown bear home to their families. (Chlaus Lotscher)*

ABOVE RIGHT: *Maggie Michaels, a Yup'ik from Bethel, deftly uses an ulu to cut king salmon her husband caught in a drift net at their fish camp on the Kuskokwim River. (Richard Montagna)*

extreme spiritual feeling I receive. At dance festivals when a member of the audience yelled 'pumyaa' (bum-e-yaw, meaning encore) I would gladly repeat the dance with all the energy I had left, to please the audience, myself and my people."

Other elements of Yup'ik culture alive and visible today come from the traditional skills of carving, skin sewing and basket making. Yup'ik people still make many cultural items for their own use, such as blackfish traps, spear points, fur boots, parkas and dance fans, as well as making them to sell to collectors of Native art. The Yup'ik have also encouraged

continuation of their language by including bilingual and Yup'ik immersion programs in their schools. The less visible aspects of Yup'ik culture, as for the other Native cultures in Alaska, are the beliefs shaping their view of the world. The missionaries did their work well in rural Alaska, converting people with a passion that has brought generations of devout followers. But at the same time, the Yup'ik, like other Natives, have recognized that their

Yup'ik children romp with a homemade sled in Bethel, regional hub near the mouth of the Kuskokwim River. In the smaller villages, youngsters curious about visitors may ply them with questions such as: "Who are you and how long are you staying?" (Don Pitcher)

ancestor's cosmology was not exclusive of Christianity, and that many of the basic values espoused by Christian doctrines were also integral to Native spirituality. Reciprocity, sharing and conscious awareness are such elements of the Yup'ik world view. "Things are not always what they seem...many possibilities exist and we are not to be indifferent to other people's needs," explains Elsie Mather, Yup'ik linguist and author of *Cauyarnariuq: A Time for Drumming* (1985). *"Everything on Ear th deser ves recognition, car e and respect."* ■

Living in Manokotak

By Anecia Lomack

Editor's note: *Anecia Lomack lives in Manokotak, a Yup'ik village of 442 people on Bristol Bay, and currently teaches 3rd and 4th grades at Manokotak School. Since becoming a certified teacher in 1982, Anecia has taught Yugtun language in the school's Bilingual Program; she also teaches English-as-a-Second-Language. She enjoys writing about her ancestors' history, and caring for her family, including her mother.*

I would like to dedicate this article to all our Elders in Alaska and especially to my mother, Betusia Alakayak, who has seen a lot of changes in her 88 years in Bristol Bay. From being a nomad in the coastal region between Dillingham and Togiak, she is now settled in the village of Manokotak on the west side of Nushagak Bay. Manokotak, which means "on the lap of," sits on the lap of Manokotak Mountain. The village did not exist until about 1947, when our ancestors decided to settle for education and church activities.

Our ancestors traveled to different areas according to seasonal subsistence activities. They traveled by foot, in *qayaqs* (kayaks) and by dog teams to where subsistence food was plentiful. My mother spent the first half of her life walking over the mountains, kayaking and using wooden skiffs on lakes, rivers and bays. She traveled for seasonal subsistence along Kulukak River, Kulukak and Nushagak bays, and along the Igushik River and smaller river cutoffs such as Anguuq and Iiyussiiq (today the commercial and subsistence fishing grounds on Nushagak Bay).

Every day was dedicated to survival and success. The prosperous family was alert to all areas of lifeskills. Weather was read through the eyes of the *elisngalria* (educated) person. Time was read according to the daylight, sun, stars, clouds, animals, fish and the seasonal changes. Harvesting of animals, plants, berries, fish, water and wood, to heat the house, was important. Cooperation, sharing and much respect for Elders and belief in the Creator were some of the many determinations that led to successful *yuuyaraq'* (way of life).

Everything was respected and taken care of with dignity. The bones of a subsisted animal were never *sagteq* (scattered). There were some animals that were never chopped, but a certain tool was used to cut them up. As my mother says, "Everything had a *qanruyun* (adage)." When the *qanruyun* was heeded, then prosperity was present. When carelessness existed, the game became scarce and hunger was present.

Beaming villagers Nancy Sharp, Anecia Lomack, Ferdinand Sharp and Nellie Gamechuk show off walrus flippers and organs. (Erik Hill, Anchorage Daily News)

Lucy Gloko (left), a past health aide, and current health aide Anuska Nicketa help see to the needs of Manokotak villagers. (Mark Dolan photo, courtesy of Bristol Bay Area Health Corp.)

Many changes have taken place in the lives of our "now old" parents and grandparents. At Kulukak, an old village on the west shore of Kulukak Bay, education was introduced but it was not a vital part of their subsistence lifestyle. At right times when the families were not so busy, they permitted their children to go to the one-room school. They also saw ships, wooden skiffs, and very, very occasionally a plane that would be awesome to the women and young children.

Now they are no longer traveling place to place. *Qasgiqs* (men's advice houses) are no longer in existence. And many of the physical jobs are no longer present. My mother and many of the other Elders often reminisce with positive memories of what used to be.

Manokotak has now existed for about 50 years. It has gone from having one church classroom to many classrooms for almost every grade. Walking has been replaced by trucks, four-wheelers, snow-gos, and even a daily school bus.

Education is now the push for many community members. Much progress has occurred for improve-ment of Manokotak students' education, such as having computers to do research papers, having a Bilingual Program, and even having a hot lunch program. I remember as an elementary student being restricted from speaking my own *Yugtun* (Yup'ik) language. I had to rely on older students who understood more and try to survive by what I saw. We are now teaching in our own *Yugtun* language from kinder-garten to fourth grade. Five Native certified teachers, including myself, teach our students.

Subsistence is still continued in our community, although many people also use *Kass'artaq* (Western style) food. In the falltime, villagers go berry picking for blackberries, cranberries and blueberries to store in freezers. They also put up lake-spawning salmon. Those with jet boats find it easy to navigate the shallow waters of the first and second lakes of Igushik River.

Breezy, sunny weather is needed for drying spawning red salmon, which take longer to dry than the ocean fresh salmon. There is an island in the first lake with fishracks used by many of the Manokotak people for drying this delicious white-skinned salmon. We call these dried salmon *tamuanaq* (the kind you chew on). When dried too long, they can get as hard as jerky. *Tamuanaqs* are a specialty dipped in seal oil or mixed in *akutaq* (Eskimo ice cream).

When moose season opens, men hunt for winter food. Fall is also a time to hunt ducks down the Igushik River. If one is lucky, a white beluga will be taken and shared with everyone in the village.

Fall 1995 was the first season in many years that walrus was hunted. Every person involved with the hunting, cutting, storing and cooking seemed very happy to have this delicious specialty.

In the wintertime, many of the men, and sometimes some brave women, will gather wood for their *maqi* (steambath). Steambath for many community members is an evening pastime, a time for bathing, relaxing and visiting with friends. I especially like *maqi* when I need stress relief, or when

I just need time away from doing home chores.

Winter is also a time to ice-fish for pike, trout and lushfish. A hole may be cut through a lake, river or pond to get any of these fish. Trout is caught in both of our nearby lakes, Amanka and Quliq. Pike and lushfish are caught in tundra ponds. Winter is also a time to hunt ptarmigan, caribou and moose and for trapping fur animals such as beaver.

In the springtime, many of the fishermen get ready for herring season in Kulukak Bay. They fish commercially for herring, and some of the women put up herring for subsistence use. During herring season, which is usually about the end of April, seals are hunted and many people dig butter clams during the lowest low tide. Ducks of all sorts are also hunted at the ocean or inside rivers.

As springtime comes to a close, king salmon are swimming in the bays. Many Manokotak people move down to Igushik, a commercial and subsistence camping village on Nushagak Bay. All able families prepare all the salmon that come in the Igushik River for their winter food supply. While getting ready for commercial openings, many of the families will put up fish, smoke

them when dried and get them ready for storing in their freezers.

At fish camp whenever time is available, many of the younger and older women gather edible green plants. It is so much fun to gather the beach greens, wild celery and sour dock.

The second week of July is when salmon berries are beginning to get ripe. Many of the women and some men will pick them.

The peak of commercial fishing season is about the Fourth of July. With the way it is celebrated in modern society, we can see fireworks and many young people enjoying the summer night visiting with friends. Fish camp season

Manokotak villagers divide shares of walrus after a successful hunt on Round Island in Bristol Bay in winter 1995. Manokotak was allowed to harvest two of 10 walrus allotted to seven area villages in the first state-approved hunt in the Walrus Islands State Game Sanctuary since the refuge was created in 1960. While the meat, organs and hide was toted to kettles and freezers, the tusks were donated to the school for carving lessons. (Erik Hill, Anchorage Daily News)

wraps up about the end of July.

The return to Manokotak is once again enjoyed more because of its luxuries — television, running water, big beds, refrigerators, freezers, electricity and other things that were beyond our reach at fish camp. Many families are beginning to get ready for school season. Those that made a profit from commercial fishing may run into Anchorage to shop and get more of their winter food, furniture and clothing. Many of the younger people and some men and women have learned to drive the city roads and know the way

to visit towns near Anchorage.

These are some touches of all-year activities that Manokotak people do. Our activities now may not be with our ancestors' nomadic subsistence lifestyle, but we certainly can reflect their dedication to the realities of life — hard work, sharing, cooperation and successfulness. We will feel good about our accomplishments and reminisce positively of our life at Manokotak. With Manokotak's economic and more Western style development, we will certainly remember what it was like in our time and life. ☐

Yup'ik Dance Masks: Stories of Culture

A group of school children gathered around the wooden *nepcetaq* mask, its smiling mouth lined with what looked like real teeth. The face had tear-shaped eye holes with a third eye pegged with teeth on its forehead. The rounded *yua*, or spirit, face emerged from a feather-studded backboard, carved to represent the universe, water, air and land. Holes in the backboard showed passages through which the animals move in their journey toward the human hunter. The mask had been crafted under direction of an *angalkuq*, a powerful person, for a special purpose — perhaps to predict the future or to call forth or show gratitude to the animals. When presented in dance, it would have appeared quite animated, symbolizing the union of the seen and unseen. Now stripped of its original use and purpose and mounted behind protective glass a century removed from its context, the mask still held its mysteries.

This particular mask is part of a greater collection of more than 200 Yup'ik dance masks in an exhibit called *Agayuliyararput* (Our Way of Making Prayer). The masks were collected from southwestern Alaska around the turn of the century by missionaries and other visitors. They wound up in museums around the world where little was known about them except where, when and by whom they were collected. Now, however, a great deal more information is known, thanks to the Alaska Yup'ik community and exhibit curator Ann Fienup-Riordan, an anthropologist well-respected for her work and writings about Yup'ik culture.

Agayuliyararput is more than simply an exhibit of objects; it is a collection of stories about the masks and Yup'ik culture as told by Yup'ik people. A committee of Yup'ik men and women worked closely with Fienup-Riordan and museum specialists.

In 1996, some of the masks returned for a time to their place of origin when the exhibit debuted in the southwestern Alaska village of Toksook Bay. More than 500 Yup'iks flew into Toksook Bay the day the exhibit opened, to see the masks, to dance and feast.

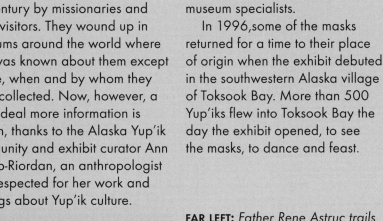

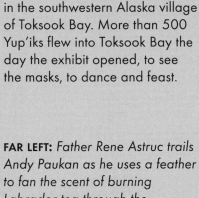

FAR LEFT: *Father Rene Astruc trails Andy Paukan as he uses a feather to fan the scent of burning Labrador tea through the Agayuliyararput exhibit during a purification ceremony at the exhibit's opening at Anchorage Museum of History and Art. (Erik Hill, Anchorage Daily News)*

LEFT: *Sheldon Jackson collected this pair of owl masks on the Lower Yukon River in the 1890s. (Barry McWayne photo, courtesy Sheldon Jackson Museum, II.H. 14 and 11)*

The exhibit then moved to the Yupiit Piciryarait Cultural Center in Bethel for a two-month stay; then to the Anchorage Museum of History and Art. From there, *Agayuliyararput* would move to Juneau and Fairbanks, then to the National Museum of the American Indian in New York and, finally, to the National Museum of Natural History at the Smithsonian Institution.

Crucial to presenting the masks was collecting stories about them from Yup'ik Elders. These Elders are some of the last survivors of a time when Yup'ik life still included masked dances in the *qasgiq*, or men's house, where the males of the winter village lived separately from the females. Pictures of the masks were taken into the homes of Yup'ik Elders by Marie Meade, a Yup'ik language specialist raised in Nunapitchuk. She recorded, then translated, their tales. Some of the Elders remembered who made particular masks; others remembered seeing the masks used; still others recalled various related happenings. Meade's 30 hours of taped interviews became the basis for many of the exhibit's interpretative materials. Condensed versions of the Elders' stories are presented in Yup'ik and English in *Kegginaqut, Kangiit-Ilu (Yup'ik*

Masks and the Stories They Tell, 1996) by Meade and Fienup-Riordan. Another essential companion book is Fienup-Riordan's comprehensive catalog, *The Living Tradition of Yup'ik Masks* (1996).

This exhibit amplifies what started in 1989 when a group of old Yup'ik masks were borrowed from the Sheldon Jackson Museum in Sitka and exhibited during a regional dance festival held in Mountain Village. Elders and community leaders had wanted to revive Yup'ik culture among young people with a display of artifacts during the festival, to show how their ancestors lived. Andy Paukan, from St. Marys, helped bring the masks back that time and worked closely with Fienup-Riordan to mount *Agayuliyararput*.

Paukan speaks about the recent exhibit's significance: "This project is important to me and, I believe, for all Yup'ik people, not because it brings the past back to us but because it may help preserve our future.... I consider it fortunate that so many well-regarded museums have fine collections of Yup'ik materials collected at an important time in our history. Certainly those who collected these items may have thought they were collecting the artifacts of a vanishing culture. However, among those of us whose

RIGHT: *Nick Charles Jr., of Bethel, applies red ochre to a newly carved mask. He demonstrated mask-making at Agayuliyararput at the Anchorage Museum of History and Art. (Walter Hays)*

LOWER RIGHT: *This nepcetaq mask was collected in 1893 by Sheldon Jackson. Nepcetaq means "something that sticks to your face" because of the way it behaved when presented in dance, according to The Living Tradition of Yup'ik Masks. (Barry McWayne photo, courtesy Sheldon Jackson Museum, II.B.8)*

forefathers were the craftsmen, these items demonstrate that we may be different, but we have not vanished."

During the opening weekend for *Agayuliyararput* at the Anchorage Museum of History and Art, contemporary carvers worked while dancers from St. Marys and Toksook Bay performed. The young Toksook dancers performed traditional dances alongside their Elders, then took the floor alone to present their own choreography, a basketball dance. With the dribbling, shooting and one-legged victory hop,

spectators could imagine Friday night games in a crowded village gym. Later, one of the men from St. Marys danced briefly with a newly carved mask, and, for a moment, the audience could almost imagine what the "real people" saw those many years ago. □

Siberian Yupik

In Alaska, Siberian Yupik is spoken exclusively on St. Lawrence Island, where almost all Native residents still speak it, and it is the first language their children learn. Siberian Yupik is a different language, mostly unintelligible to speakers of Central Yup'ik, and is also spoken by a small group of Natives on the southern tip of the Chukotsk Peninsula in Russia.

The Siberian Yupik of St. Lawrence Island rarely engage in inland activities and depend mostly on marine mammals for food and cultural traditions. They hunt bowhead whales from open skin boats powered with sails, dividing up the meat and fat following customs that prescribe certain parts to the hunters, their families and other villagers. Like Alaska's other Native people, they, too, take advantage of the latest technology and use metal boats with outboard motors, snow machines and four-wheeled all-terrain vehicles when suitable. □

BELOW, LEFT: *Wooden umiak frames, turned upside-down to store for winter on St. Lawrence Island, are popular with young climbers, as this boy in Savoonga demonstrates. (Jon R. Nickles)*

BELOW: *Alaska Natives, including the people of St. Lawrence Island, are finding new economies in tourism. The villagers in Gambell welcome visitors, many of whom come in tour groups and talk with whaling captains, watch ivory carvers, go birdwatching or, as these visitors are doing, inspect walrus skins stretched on a frame for an umiak cover. (Harry Walker)*

FACING PAGE: The Siberian Yupik people of St. Lawrence Island depend on marine mammals for food. Whaling has changed little in recent decades, although hunters today observe strict conservation quotas. This photo from the 1960s shows villagers from Gambell stripping whale skin and blubber, a harvest practice still used. (Steve McCutcheon)

Inupiat

The Inupiat Eskimos are the farthest north Alaska Natives. They include bowhead whale hunters living along the Chukchi and Beaufort coasts of the Arctic Ocean, who launch skin-covered boats into ice-choked waters to chase, harpoon and drag ashore 60-ton behemoths. They include polar bear, seal and walrus hunters of Kotzebue Sound and the Seward Peninsula. They include salmon fishermen, reindeer herders and caribou hunters along the coast, inland rivers, or in the arctic tundra of the central Brooks Range. They include women skilled in sewing skins into boat covers, who can fashion fur garments to protect against instant frostbite in howling winter winds, who spend days in their kitchens cooking up feasts of traditional, ceremonial and Western foods to feed entire villages.

Alaska's Inupiat live in many small villages where their ancestors have lived for centuries, and they live in larger towns built atop ancient trading sites. More than 12,600 Inupiat people

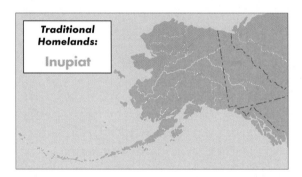

Traditional Homelands: **Inupiat**

live today in their traditional homelands — the face-shaped northwest corner of Alaska and along the North Slope. Inupiat people also are among the 6,000 Eskimos living in Anchorage, and more than 1,500 Eskimos in Fairbanks; the census does not distinguish between Inupiat and Yup'ik.

Barrow, the northernmost city in Alaska, is one of those old Inupiat trading sites. With a population of 4,100, more than half of whom are Inupiat, Barrow is home to Arctic Slope Regional Corp., perhaps the richest Native

corporation in the state, and headquarters for the North Slope Borough, one of the wealthiest local governments in Alaska by virtue of property taxes on North Slope oil field developments. It's a place where whaling captains are as comfortable in the corporation's mirrored-glass office tower as in their skin *umiats* on the ocean. Tucked down around the coast off Bering Strait sits Kotzebue, a largely Inupiat town of nearly 3,600 people. Kotzebue serves as the regional and commercial center for northwest Alaska. The Inupiat region extends south to encompass the Seward Peninsula to Unalakleet River. It includes the gold-mine

FACING PAGE: *Many people from Anaktuvuk Pass, an Inupiat village in the Brooks Range, depend on caribou for food. Here, Jenny Paneak cuts caribou meat at fall hunting camp about 15 miles from the village. (Henry P. Huntington)*

town of Nome with about 3,500 people, about half of whom are Inupiat.

Westernization has come to Inupiat villages in various forms and degrees during the last two decades, blending with remnants of earlier times. Many efforts are being made in Inupiat towns and villages to strengthen cultural connections, such as Inupiaq language and culture programs in the schools. In Barrow, for instance, signs throughout the city are written in Inupiaq as well as English, and the local radio station broadcasts some programs in Inupiaq.

"Our Elders have always told us that if we lose our language, we'll lose our culture," says Fannie Akpik, head of the Inupiat studies program at Ilisagvik College in Barrow. Along with teaching, she broadcasts the Inupiaq "word of the day" over radio station KBRW, which also airs an Inupiaq story hour each weeknight. Most fluent speakers of Inupiaq are Elders or middle-aged adults.

Inupiat people living in Alaska's largest cities such as Anchorage, like other Alaska Natives in urban settings, may be more physically isolated

from traditional lifestyles. A group of 25 Inupiat women from the North Slope living and working in Anchorage during the 1980s and 1990s talked about this with researcher Nancy Fogel-Chance. To maintain their cultural identity, the women purposefully maintained an important aspect of Inupiat culture — sharing. This included frequent visiting among members of small groups to help each other with transportation, childcare, food, finances, practical skills and wisdom.

"We just do what is needed," one of the women explained.

Fogel-Chance elaborates. "A direct request for assistance would be improper," she writes in the journal *Arctic.* "People are not always able to provide help. It is a serious breach of etiquette to put someone in the position of having to say 'no.' Making a need known is usually done indirectly. Additionally, the reciprocity is a long-term matter...it is rude for someone to reciprocate immediately.... Sharing does not offer a means of getting ahead, nor is it a way of redistributing scarce goods. Mostly it wards off the atomization of urban Western

This summer aerial shows a portion of Barrow, or Utqiagvik, *the northernmost Alaska Native settlement. The red-roofed buildling is the new school; the causeway leads across the lagoon to the part of town known as Browerville. Less than a century ago, people here still lived in semisubterranean sod houses; today buildings are elevated on pilings atop gravel pads, a modern method of arctic construction in permafrost and wetlands. (Jon R. Nickles)*

life by reinforcing a sense of 'Inupiat-ness.'"

The Inupiat people can trace their ancestors to the beginning of time in their stories; archaeologists have traced them back thousands of years in Alaska, to camping and trading sites used by some of the first Inupiat ancestors to enter from Asia. One of their oldest sites is Onion Portage on the Kobuk River. Archaeological finds in northern Alaska show a progression of cultural adaptations and change that includes hunting large mammals, netting fish and spearing caribou. About 2,500 years ago, Inupiat ancestors started hunting seals and other sea mammals. Whaling technologies appeared about 1,500 years ago. One of the oldest whaling settlements was at Point Hope. Coastal camps grew into large settlements, as people cooperated to harvest the large sea mammals. Eventually, someone started fishing with hooks and lines, and people moved inland to live by lakes and rivers. The introduction of the sinew bow from Asia gave new efficiency to caribou hunting. About 500 years ago, people started harnessing dogs to sleds to work.

Elmer Goodwin, a 55-year-old Inupiat living in Kotzebue, said that as a youngster his grandparents taught him by example such things as setting snares for rabbits and using dog sleds. "When outboards (motors) came, they taught me how to do that. Then snow

BELOW: *Ellen Paneak of Kotzebue has been flying planes through rural Alaska for about 15 years. She also carves ivory. (Barbara Willard)*

BELOW RIGHT: *Birchbark basketry is a traditional art in some Inupiat villages, as demonstrated by Jane Young in 1984 in Kobuk. Baskets are made for sale, for personal use and as gifts. (Roz Goodman)*

LEFT: *An Inupiat family returns to Barrow from fall seal hunting. (Chris Wooley)*

FACING PAGE: *Women gather at Burton Rexford's house in Barrow to sew bearded seal skins into an umiak cover. The edges of two skins are overlapped about an inch, and each edge is whipped down with stitches that go only halfway through the underlying skin. This is a water-proofing measure so needle holes do not penetrate both skins completely. Five to seven skins are needed for one cover. When the women finish, it will be stretched over the wooden umiak frame. (Henry P. Huntington)*

Arctic. The group was recently featured on national radio, during a broadcast from Anchorage of Garrison Keillor's "A Prairie Home Companion." Radio listeners heard their drumming and singing; the studio audience saw their dancing.

Drummer Martin Woods told about seal hunting — how the hunter would shoot the seal, use a grappling hook to pull it from the water before it could sink, gut it, pay respects to its spirit, then bring it to the village for a celebration. He said he was excited about his first whale hunt with relatives from Barrow. Although he grew up spending summers in fish camp, he now has a job in town. "I'm like a city boy. I collect a paycheck. I pay taxes like everybody else." He explained how whales are hunted today with exploding harpoon tips, which more quickly kills the animal. This, he joked, "alleviates having to go on a Nantucket sleigh ride until they tire, jump on their back

machines came. There's been a lot of changes since I've been alive — modern houses, telephones, cars in the village."

Goodwin lived in Los Angeles for 11 years after graduating from high school. He wanted to experience "life with white man in his own environment." He attended welding school, worked as a construction foreman and clerked in a furniture store. But he missed "my people, my Native food...seals, fish, dried fish and meat. And I missed my language. There was nobody to talk to down there." Each summer, he returned to his village to visit. Finally, he returned for good.

Today, Goodwin works in Kotzebue for the Northern Alaska Native Association, the regional corporation for 11 villages in the area. He coordinates Camp *Sivuniigvik*, "the place to make plans for the future." Elders at the summer camp teach language and survival skills to school-age youths as a way to reinforce Inupiat customs and traditions. It's held on the Kobuk River between Kotzebue and Noorvik.

Inupiat Elders, adults and young people in Kotzebue also come together as the Northern Lights Dancers, a well-traveled group that performs traditional Inupiat songs and dances in summer at the NANA Museum of the

and pierce their heart with a lance."

Native subsistence bowhead whaling has undergone numerous modifications in recent decades. The International Whaling Commission determines a quota for hunting, based on the strength of the whale population. The Alaska Eskimo Whaling Commission then divides that quota among the whaling villages, allotting each a certain number of "strikes," or

attempts. The AEWC is composed of Natives from each of the eight Inupiat whaling villages and the two Siberian Yupik villages on St. Lawrence Island.

Whaling figures prominently in the history of the Inupiat region. In the late 1840s, American whalers sailed to the Bering Strait region in the first big wave of outsiders. They brought trade goods and employed some Inupiat whalers seasonally. They also brought disease and alcohol. Although few whalers settled in the region, their impact was long-lived.

Today subsistence whaling remains a strong and visible aspect of Inupiat culture. Hunting these large creatures from small craft in the

polar seas is dangerous and requires immeasurable seafaring skills and cooperation between boats. The entire community spends months preparing gear, clothing and food for the crews. Once landed, the whale is divided among crew members, and shares are given to Elders, families without hunters and sometimes sent to relatives in cities. Throughout the year, whale is shared at festivals, holidays and other special occasions.

Even though whaling is closely associated with Inupiat culture, the majority of Inupiat villages are not directly involved with hunting bowheads. However hunting for beluga whales, walrus, and bearded and ringed seals is important to most of the villages. Spring harvests in the Kotzebue basin focus on bearded and ringed seals off Cape Krusenstern and Cape Espenberg. Beluga hunters pitch tents along the beach at Elephant Point on Eschscholtz Bay, where belugas feed on spawning smelt.

What Inupiat people do largely depends on the season and available resources. In addition

FAR LEFT: *On the ice outside Barrow, a jubilant Edward Itta is about to land the first whale of his career as a whaling captain. Here he shouts "walk away," the instruction for people to start pulling the ropes attached to the whale's tail. The use of a block-and-tackle helps the crew pull the whale onto the ice. (Henry P. Huntington)*

LEFT: *The women of a whaling crew prepare uunaalik (boiled fresh whale blubber, skin and meat) to feed the men doing the butchering. (Henry P. Huntington)*

to sea mammals, villagers may harvest caribou, polar and grizzly bears, musk oxen, whitefish, tomcod, salmon, smelt, arctic char, waterfowl, berries and wild vegetables. Subsistence activities are culturally important and often provide most of a family's nutritional needs.

BELOW: *Inupiat people used baleen, a bony substance taken from the mouth of a bowhead whale, for buckets, scoops and sled runners; it was sought by commercial whalers for manufacture as corset stays and umbrella ribs. Baskets coiled from thin strips of baleen were first made in the early 1900s. This baleen basket with its ivory finial was made by the late George Omnik of Point Hope, a master of the art. Today, his sons James Sr. and John and his grandson James Jr. continue the tradition. (Steve McCutcheon)*

RIGHT: *Many villagers get around by snow machines or four-wheelers, depending on the season, but on this winter day a woman in Unalakleet prefers skis. (Roz Goodman)*

Subsistence can be a full-time job, but many people also need cash wage employment to pay expenses. They find work, often seasonal, at local schools, in government and small businesses, in commercial fishing and construction, and in the North Slope oil fields or the big Red Dog zinc mine near Kotzebue.

Some Inupiat herd reindeer, domestic cousins to caribou. Reindeer were introduced as a food source in northwestern Alaska in the 1890s by Sheldon Jackson, then superintendent of education for Alaska. A law passed in 1937 restricted reindeer ownership to Natives, and today about a dozen permit holders — individuals, families and Native corporations — manage 23,000 to 28,000 reindeer on the Seward Peninsula. Reindeer handling blends with subsistence activities. In spring, the herders monitor calving. In June, using helicopters to round up the herd, they harvest antlers for mostly Asian markets. In early winter, the herders on snow machines catch and butcher the steers. Much of the meat is processed commercially and sold as sausage.

In Anaktuvuk Pass in the central Brooks Range, caribou is the primary food. Many items are made from the skins, including masks. In earlier times, people walked from Anaktuvuk Pass to the coast to trade caribou skins and fur pelts for seal oil. Today traveling by airplane, people take great pleasure in sharing their subsistence foods and handiwork with friends and relatives in other villages.

A big trade fair with ancient traditions has once again become a much-anticipated annual event. The festival, *Kivgiq*, is held midwinter and draws upwards of 600 people to dance, eat, trade items, sell crafts, exchange gifts, tell stories and play games. It is not advertised to tourists; the hotels are filled with people from the region's villages. "It is a time to draw the community together," said Marie Adams, of the North Slope Borough, which sponsors *Kivgiq*. After hearing Elders reminisce about the old "messenger feast," last held in 1914, Borough Mayor George Ahmaogak sparked its return in 1988. "It was revived to help strengthen people's identity and culture," said Adams. "Our philosophy is that when people have a strong sense of themselves, they are less likely to get into trouble. This has helped people feel good about themselves and their culture." ∎

ABOVE: *Beverly (left) and Samantha Thomas peek out the window as the day's wash dries in Buckland, a small Inupiat village near the head of Kotzebue Sound. (Danny Daniels)*

RIGHT: *Tommy Pikok and his grandson, Gilford "Mongoyuk" Pikok, perform with the Nuvukmiut Dancers of Barrow during the 1995 Inuit Circumpolar Conference in Nome. The ICC represents Inuits around the polar rim on environmental and political concerns. (Roz Goodman)*

A Time for Whaling

By Shelia Frankson

Editor's Note: *Sheila graduated in May 1996 from Tikigaq High School in Point Hope, where she lives with her mother Susie Frankson and youngest brother. Her father Clement lives in Barrow. Sheila plans to attend Sheldon Jackson College in Sitka. "Making that decision was very hard. I wasn't sure if I wanted to go away. I wasn't sure if college was for me," says Sheila. "Even though I'm scared, I'll give it a try. Then I'll know what it's like to experience the outside world on my own."*

My name is Sheila Frankson. I'm a 17-year-old Inupiat Eskimo from Point Hope. My village of about 650 people is located on the northwest coast of Alaska. It is one of the state's oldest villages.

Springtime is our whaling season. A couple years ago, I had my first experience out on the ice during whaling season with Calvin and Irma Oktollik. Even though I have lived in Point Hope all my life and join every year in the work and celebration of whaling season, I'd never actually gone out to stay at a whaling camp. I was really excited!

During winter, snow falls and the wind blows. It gets really cold — temperatures reach minus 60, dropping to 80 and 90 below zero with wind chill — and the ocean freezes. The Arctic Ocean has a permanent frozen mass called pack ice that can freeze to new ice during winter. Some ice may be light blue and some may be plain white. When you go out on the frozen ocean, you see a lot of big and small pieces of ice on top of each other.

To get ready for whaling, the men break trail through these jumbles of ice. They use certain tools such as ice picks, axes and shovels. When they return to set their tent, they'll know which way to go. They make a trail all the way to the open lead — a place where the ice has broken apart into an open channel. The whales, who need air to breathe, travel these leads through the ice to their calving grounds. An open lead is usually several miles out from shore, although some years the lead can be seen from town.

While the men break trail, the ladies sew seal skins together to make covers for the umiaks, the skin boats used for whaling. They sew the skins together in a particular way with ivory needles and thick thread, so the skins won't rip apart while the men are in the boat pursuing a whale.

We get to our tents at whaling camp on snow machines pulling wooden sleds. Back in the old days (before the late 1960s), we didn't have cars or snow machines. All we had were dogs and sleds for transportation. The village men still make the sleds to haul gear and umiaks out to the ice and bring *maktak* (muktuk) and whale meat back. *Maktak* is the blubber and skin of the whale that my people consider a delicacy to eat.

When I go out on the ice, I have certain chores to do. They include washing dishes after every meal and keeping the area around and inside the tent clean. Some days, if the *boyars* (young boys who help around the tent) are not around, I also help cut up driftwood and seal blubber to burn in the stove, and get snow to melt for drinking

Sheila Frankson stands beside a skin-covered umiak used in whaling. (Courtesy of Public Information Office, North Slope Borough)

and washing if we are running out.

The *boyar* also stays up during the night and tends the stove while the hunters sleep. When the whalers wake up, they go back out to the wind breakers and look for whales. Wind breakers are pieces of ice that have been set up at the edge of the lead. When you look into the open water from behind a breaker, you can see if the whales are passing by.

If the water closes up with ice and the lead disappears, the crew members return to the village to wait for a lead to open again.

When you go out on the ice, you can't use anything red because the color will scare the whales. You also have to wear warm clothing. When you're out there, it gets cold even though some days are a little warm. You need such things as ski pants, boots, gloves or mittens, a couple pairs of socks, Eskimo jacket (parka with ruff) and a hat.

After one of the crews catches a whale, everybody starts yelling with excitement! Usually it takes at least a day to cut up a whale. The whale is harvested on the ice where it was landed. Back in

People of Point Hope still celebrate the enduring tradition of Nalukataq in much the same way as they did here in the 1970s. (Steve McCutcheon)

town, the families of the crew and the captain give out candy to celebrate. Everybody is welcome to take some. It's a tradition that's been going on for many years.

Whaling season ends for one of two reasons. Either we have reached the quota our village is given by the Alaska Eskimo Whaling Commission or the ice is getting too rotten to stay out safely.

After whaling season is over, we wait for June to have a feast called *Nalukataq*. We go out on the tundra outside of town by the whalebones that have been set up for a long time. This is the traditional place for our *Nalukataq*. Here we serve food and give a share of the whales to everyone who comes. It's a time for gathering and talking. People from different villages usually come to Point Hope every year for *Nalukataq* to celebrate with their friends and relatives.

On the first day, a village Elder such as Seymore Tuzroyluke says a little prayer before anyone eats. Then everybody eats, visits awhile and goes home. The next day, they return and eat again. Afterward, they Eskimo dance and do the blanket toss.

The blanket is seal skins sewn together with rope handles around the edge. One person gets on top of the skin blanket while other people grab the handles and bounce it to throw that person up in the air. While up in the air, that person moves his or her legs as if running. Some people throw candy into the air while they're being tossed, and everybody tries to get all the candy they can. It's one of the things that I like watching (other than basketball!).

As a teenager, I'm slowly learning what it was like in the old days. But as I get older, I realize that not being able to speak my Native language, *Inupiaq*, is a problem. I want to learn *Inupiaq*, but I find it hard to understand. I want to be able to communicate in *Inupiaq* with our Elders in Point Hope, to have them tell me what it was like living in the old days. When our Elders talk in *Inupiaq*, I listen to small words that I know, and I try to understand what they're saying. I'm hoping some day I will be able to talk to our Elders using my traditional language.

Our language and our traditions mean a lot to our Elders, and I know that they want to see that we learn it. On the other hand, having to get everything ready for whaling and *Nalukataq* isn't that easy.

Although it's hard work, we Inupiat never give up. We do our best and if it means we have to keep on trying, then that's what we do. We'll do it over and over until we feel we've gotten it right. ☐

RIGHT: *Whaling Capt. Joe Frankson, Sheila Frankson's uncle, was photographed at Point Hope 20 years ago with this section of baleen. Pieces of the baleen were distributed as gifts. (Steve McCutcheon)*

FAR RIGHT: *Whaling crews tow their umiak through a trail in the ice to open water. (Steve McCutcheon)*

Athabaskan

Alaska's Athabaskan people occupy the largest geographic area with the most diverse environments of any of Alaska's Native groups. Alaska's broad Interior is usually identified as the Athabaskan heartland, but their homelands stretch from the Brooks Range south past the Alaska Range to Lake Iliamna, Cook Inlet and the Kenai Peninsula.

The territory's mountains, rolling uplands, boreal spruce forests, valleys, lakes, wetlands and coastal habitats all play a part in Athabaskan culture and lore. But perhaps most pivotal to the Athabaskan lifestyle have been the region's many waterways, including the mighty Yukon, Kuskokwim, Koyukuk, Tanana, Susitna and Copper river systems. For centuries, Athabaskans have traveled, traded, fished, hunted, trapped and lived along these rivers and their tributaries. The rivers also brought explorers, traders, missionaries and miners, opening Athabaskan country to an era of change still unfolding.

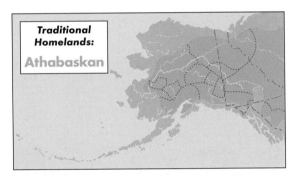

Traditional Homelands: Athabaskan

Athabaskans represent one of the most widespread linguistic groups among Natives in North America. They extend from Alaska's Arctic through Canada to the Mexican border, and include the Navajo and Apache of the American Southwest.

About 11,700 Athabaskans live in Alaska, many of them in remote villages accessible only by airplanes and boats, or snowmachines and dog sleds in winter. Even so, most villages have satellite communications, including television. Village-operated diesel-powered generators provide electricity, but few homes have running water or flush toilets. Tribal councils are an important form of village governance, and Athabaskan villages have been leaders in Native Alaska in asserting tribal powers under federal law.

People in Athabaskan villages do a variety of things to make a living and obtain cash to buy ammunition and gasoline for boats and four-wheelers for subsistence activities. Some people hold government jobs such as teachers' aides and public health aides. Some summers, young adults can earn a decent income fighting forest fires on public lands; however, a recent shift in hiring practices favors professional "hot shot" crews from Outside over villagers. Many people

FACING PAGE: *Steven Tritt of Arctic Village cooks whitefish, an important subsistence food, at camp. (Karen Jettmar)*

fish commercially for salmon and work construction. A growing list of communities — including Stevens Village, Huslia and Tyonek — market themselves as tourist destinations for visitors interested in Native lifestyles.

Subsistence hunting and fishing remain central to Athabaskan culture. People depend on salmon, whitefish, grayling, tomcod, moose, caribou, bear, beaver, hare, birds, berries and edible plants. Upland villages not located on major salmon rivers rely substantially on migrating caribou and resident populations of moose.

"I live in Fairbanks and I still live off the land," says Amy Van Hatten, who grew up in Galena. She sends fishnets and canning jars to relatives in the villages; they send her salmon. She describes her backyard with its smoke-house as like a fish camp. She regularly dines on moose. She remembers a business trip to Washington, D.C., when her craving for moose meat was insatiable. "My physical nature depends on it," she says.

"We are a very rich culture, with a lot to be proud of. I go back (to the village) as often as I can. My roots are strong."

Athabaskan people often identify themselves according to their home village. In a broader sense, the villages fall into linguistic territories corresponding to the 11 Athabaskan languages traditionally spoken in Alaska — Ahtna, Dena'ina, Deg Hit'an, Holikachuk, Koyukon, Upper Kuskokwim, Tanana, Tanacross, Upper Tanana, Han and Gwich'in. These languages are, for the most part, not mutually intelligible, and most have more than one dialect. The greatest numbers of Native speakers are found among the Gwich'in and Koyukon — the largest of all of Alaska's Athabaskan groups. The number of fluent speakers grows smaller each year; most are Elders. In only the most tradi-tional villages do children speak the language although fewer are learning in recent years.

Now for some far distant past: The Athabaskan ancestors, whom linguists call the NaDene, were among the latter waves of people to come into Alaska from Asia. Small groups, perhaps following herds of bison, elk, caribou and mammoths, crossed the Bering Sea land bridge exposed by lower ice-age ocean levels. These ancient people also fished and hunted small mammals and birds, according to archaeological finds of late ice-age camps, such as the Broken Mammoth site on the Tanana River. Some linguists suggest that eastcentral Alaska and Canada's Yukon Territory served as the NaDene homeland. As groups of NaDene went their separate ways over time, different languages and cultures evolved including Athabaskan, Eyak and Tlingit.

Until about the last 100 years, the Athabaskan people in Alaska lived a semi-nomadic existence, moving seasonally from

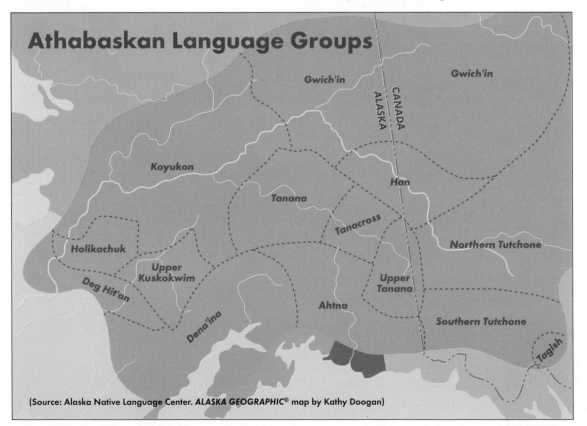

Athabaskan Language Groups

Gwich'in

Gwich'in

CANADA
ALASKA

Koyukon

Han

Tanana

Tanacross

Northern Tutchone

Holikachuk

Upper Kuskokwim

Deg Hit'an

Upper Tanana

Dena'ina

Ahtna

Southern Tutchone

Tagish

(Source: Alaska Native Language Center. **ALASKA GEOGRAPHIC**® map by Kathy Doogan)

camp to camp. They lived in small groups, often composed of extended family and led by the most skillful and accomplished hunter, usually a man with considerable spiritual powers. Generally the groups remained independent of each other as they moved about, building temporary shelters with branches and moose hides. Sometimes they built more permanent structures from bark, moss or sod.

In some places, the Athabaskans adopted technology from their neighbors; for instance the Deg Hit'an in southwestern Alaska borrowed ideas from the Yup'ik, such as masked dancing and communal structures with benches and fire pits for winter camps. The Dena'ina — the only Athabaskans in Alaska to live on saltwater and hunt sea mammals such as sea lions and beluga whales — used kayaklike boats

Martha Russell (left) and Cora Christian prepare caribou meat for roasting in Arctic Village during the 1991 International Indian Treaty Council meeting. Gwich'in culture depends on the Porcupine caribou herd, which migrates through their region to calve on the coastal plain in the Arctic National Wildlife Refuge. The Gwich'in adamantly oppose oil drilling there because of potential disruption to the caribou.(George Matz)

FACING PAGE: *Silas Alexander and stepson Dax Bifelt position a new fish wheel on the Chena River outside the Native Village Museum at Alaskaland in Fairbanks. Alexander, of Fort Yukon, made the fish wheel from spruce saplings. Baskets on each side, turned by the current, scoop fish into a holding bin. This technology, introduced to Alaska about 100 years ago by miners, is widely used today by Natives on Interior rivers for subsistence salmon fishing.* (Colleen Herning-Wickens)

RIGHT: *Melissa Roemer, a long-time resident of upper Kuskokwim River villages, was well-known for her beadwork and knitting. She passed away at her home in McGrath in 1992 at age 77.* (Richard Montagna)

FAR RIGHT: *Dora Stokes of Nikolai sprints to win a snowshoe race, part of a three-day* Hutenodinech *(we're having a good time) carnival. Held each March to celebrate spring's arrival, the festival draws upper Kuskokwim River villagers to compete in wood cutting, fire building, marksmanship and other traditional skills needed for life in the Bush.* (Richard Montagna)

common to the Alutiiq, who frequented Cook Inlet to hunt and raid Dena'ina villages.

Despite their relative autonomy, various Athabaskan groups would come together each year for trade and festivities; sometimes they would trade with the Eskimos. For instance, the Ahtna came down the Matanuska River valley to trade with the Dena'ina on Cook Inlet; the Gwich'in who settled Arctic Village used to trek

300 miles through the Brooks Range to the Arctic coast, to trade sinew, wolverine skins and spruce pitch with the Inupiat for seal oil. The community of Tanana still holds a festival each June to commemorate ancient Athabaskan trade gatherings at nearby *Nuchalawoya*, a site between the Tanana and Yukon rivers.

In the late 1700s, Europeans started appearing in Athabaskan territory. The Russians ventured into Dena'ina territory on Cook Inlet and Ahtna country on the lower Copper River in the 1780s, then filtered west to the Kuskokwim River and by the 1840s had penetrated the lower Yukon River. Meanwhile, Hudson's Bay Co. fur traders floated down the Yukon River out of Canada, establishing Fort Yukon in 1847. The traders introduced material goods, guns, and Western foods such as sugar, tea and alcohol. Hudson's Bay Co.

traders also brought fiddles; their French-Canadian and Scottish tunes were adopted by the Gwich'in and Koyukon. A distinct style of Athabaskan fiddle playing evolved, additionally influenced by string music brought later by other outsiders. Today, that musical legacy is enjoyed at village dances and each November in Fairbanks, during the Athabaskan Old-Time Fiddling Festival.

The Athabaskans also encountered military expeditions, missionaries and gold prospectors who fanned out along the Interior rivers. In more than one instance, Athabaskans saved the newcomers from starvation or freezing by sharing their food, fires and knowledge of the land. Lt. Henry Allen, who mapped the Copper,

BELOW: *Danny Lee, 14, of Arctic Village, singed this arctic ground squirrel over fire to remove its hair, then boiled it to feed his dogs. Lee traps squirrels by his greenhouse to keep them from gnawing through the plastic and eating corn, tomatoes and beans growing inside. He said occasionally he'll eat squirrels caught in the mountains, but those around the village feed mostly on garbage and taste bad. (Karen Jettmar)*

RIGHT: *Shirley Phillips helps her grandmother, the late Ruth Koktelash of Nondalton, untangle net at fish camp. (Roz Goodman)*

Tanana and Koyukuk rivers, wrote admiringly in 1885 of a boat — "one of the hardiest small crafts I have ever seen"— made for his crew by an Ahtna on the Copper. The man bound willow shoots with rawhide strings and covered the frame in moose hides sewed with sinew.

On the Yukon River, the Roman Catholics established a mission at Holy Cross and Nulato and the Episcopalians at Anvik. These and other missionaries encouraged the Athabaskans to establish year-round villages, so their children could be formally educated in mission schools.

That's how the village of Old Minto originated on the east bank of the Tanana River, said Robert Charlie. His grandfather, Chief Charlie, settled his band there in 1913, at the behest of the preachers. Even so, the people continued going to fishing and hunting camps. Robert Charlie said his parents usually

came back to the village during the school year; he attended through fifth grade. In 1970, after five consecutive years of flooding, the villagers relocated 20 miles north to higher ground on the Tolovana River.

Robert Charlie left the village as a young man to see how other people lived. He moved to Tanacross where he worked several years as postmaster, then to Fairbanks where he worked on the military bases and later for Tanana Chiefs Conference, the nonprofit health and social services agency for the Interior. Eight years ago, Charlie set up the nonprofit Cultural Heritage Education Institute. His goal: to bring people together and offer opportunities for Athabaskan youth to learn more about their culture. "By understanding how their people have lived, they can find their own way better," he says.

Each summer, the institute sponsors Athabaskan cultural camps at Old Minto where Elders share traditional knowledge with Natives and non-Natives. Some of the camps are geared toward young people; others are for teachers to acquaint them with the cultural background of Native students in villages or urban areas. One of the institute's newest projects is documenting Athabaskan place names and stories for locations in the Minto Flats.

A number of similar cultural revitalization efforts are going on throughout Athabaskan country.

"Typical of a lot of indigenous cultures in mainstream America, there's a growing concern about our culture adapting to change," says Will Mayo, president of Tanana Chiefs. "There are tremendous pressures from outside forces on the Athabaskan culture. The people recognize that cultures are dynamic and changing, but the question is: Are they changing in ways we can control and manage?

"Some of the deep aspects of our culture are disappearing.... Language is the real obvious one. The only people who speak fluently are the Elders, and even they say few know the 'high language.' You can imagine the loss that represents to the depth and understanding of our culture. But also the ancient skills — how people live, the clothing and crafts, the making and use of tools and hunting weapons. And storytelling, the method of transmitting cultural standards and values. People are concerned that television is becoming the storyteller, passing on values, principles and mores that aren't Athabaskan.

"Yet I go to villages and see children with strong cultural values...young people who know old songs and dances and cultural practices. Our culture is strongest in the villages where children are with their parents, where their parents are teaching them daily about their culture.... Even in my home in the city we practice the culture in ways we don't even notice, because it's bred into us...in the way we talk about animals and the simple process of going out to hunt, about the way you should conduct yourself, what's right and wrong, what to stay away from, what to pursue."

Several years ago as a featured speaker during the Alaska Federation of Natives annual meeting, Mayo surprised the crowd with a flamboyant demonstration of cultural pride. "Someone has suggested we should put away our beads and feathers and move on," Mayo

told the gathering. "I say that we need to remember who we are. I say it's time for us maybe to put away the suit jackets and ties!" With that, he stripped off his coat and tie and put on a beaded necklace, moosehide vest and gloves trimmed in beaver fur. "It's time maybe to put something aside, OK, but it is not our culture. It is not our pride." Then Mayo jumped over the speaker's table onto the stage where Peter John from Minto, the 92-year-old traditional chief of Interior Athabaskans, was seated with his wife, Elsie. Mayo began dancing and singing a celebration song from his home village of Tanana. As he sang in Koyukon, people in the audience from Interior villages joined along, cheered on by the hundreds of other Natives and observers in the convention hall. "It touched a chord," Mayo said later. "People really responded." ■

In the photo at left, Chief Andrew Isaac, traditional chief of Interior Athabaskans, posed in traditional regalia at his Dot Lake home shortly before his death in 1990. Hundreds of people attended the memorial potlatch (above), held for him the following year in Tanacross, where moosehead soup, a favorite potlatch food, was served. Chief Isaac was succeeded by Chief Peter John of Minto. (Both by Roy Corral)

People of the Yukon Flats

By Velma Wallis

Editor's Note: *Velma Wallis sends this dispatch from her two-room cabin at the junction of the Yukon and Porcupine rivers in Fort Yukon. Award-winning author of Two Old Women (1993) and Bird Girl and the Man Who Followed the Sun (1996), in which she retells Gwich'in Athabaskan legends of courage and survival, Wallis is also the mother of two busy youngsters.*

It is said that 10,000 years ago the Gwich'in people were one of the many groups who traveled over the land bridge connecting Asia to North America. The Gwich'in arrived and settled in the flatlands. We have endured.

The Gwich'in people live a simple yet complex life based around a belief that we cannot survive without each other. All of our hunting techniques and spiritual beliefs are surrounded by this philosophy. The Gwich'in used to build huge round fences to corral moose or caribou, which they brought down inside the fence. They worked together to do this. In the same way, the Gwich'in people have always tried to stick together despite their adversities.

Before the Westerners arrived, our lives depended solely upon moose, caribou, ducks, fish, beaver, muskrats, porcupine and other animals. We developed an almost religious attitude toward these animals, for without them our lives would be threatened. That is why we always use the word "respect," because back then without respect, we could become careless and perish.

In addition to the animals, we used other raw materials for many different purposes. For instance, we used birch bark and spruce roots to make containers to cook in or store berries in. Canoes also were made with huge pieces of birch bark bound together with young spruce roots and sealed with spruce sap. Willow and spruce were used to make fish traps, snowshoes and bows and arrows. Tanned moose skins and furs were used for summer and winter clothing, and plant-dyed porcupine quills embellished our attire.

The Gwich'in developed customs that shaped and dictated our lives. Our culture included rituals, such as dancing, and religious practices and beliefs that interacted with the animals and land.

Then came the time when the Gwich'in's world changed completely. My grandmother told of the time when her band first heard that Hudson's Bay Co. fur traders had arrived on the banks of the Yukon River, in 1847, at what is now known as Fort Yukon. They had come out of Canada. She said her people were upriver,

Author Velma Wallis holds daughter Laura Brianna at Fort Yukon, a commercial and transportation hub for Athabaskan villages in the region. (Erik Hill, Anchorage Daily News)

in the area of what later became known as Circle City, when one of their scouts arrived and told them about these fur traders.

My grandmother's people packed up their things and went down immediately. There they met the traders and as time passed my grandmother traded in her moose-skin dress for one made of calico, and the hunters traded in their bows and arrows for guns and powder. After contact with the Western world, many of our meaningful rituals were wiped out and remain only a dim memory in our Elders' minds.

Later when Alaska was purchased by the United States from Russia in 1867, the Canadian fur traders left Fort Yukon. The Gwich'in people continued living in the settlement, which they called *Gwichyaa Zhee*.

In the short time since, many things have happened. My grandmother's daughter Nina told me about the time she remembered when diseases arrived in our area and decimated a third of our population. She said, "At first when people died, they had funerals and people wept for their lost ones. Later, about 10 times a day they carried dead people to the graveyards, and people no longer cried."

But the Gwich'in people, like other Athabaskans and Alaska Natives, continued on. We have tried to keep up with the many changes brought by Western culture, some of which have made subsistence lifestyles easier. Yet others have made life more complicated, as people fall to addictions such as alcoholism.

Our town has gone through many different people, who have moved on or met their demise. We have seen a major hospital come and go. We have seen many different restaurants, stores, airlines and even an Air Force base. Today we have commuter airlines flying to our town out of Fairbanks. We have two stores, a post office, two restaurants and 750 people.

On Dec. 17, 1971, the Alaska Native Claims Settlement Act passed into law, and the Gwich'in people began to reclaim not only their lands but their lives. Our people began to remember their dances, their songs, their stories. They began to regain their former strength and pride. Slowly, a sobriety movement began to spread, not only through the Yukon flatlands but throughout Alaska. I remember a quote by one of the many sobriety counselors who passed through our area: "Without sobriety, there is no ball game."

Beadwork adorns moosehide moccasins trimmed in beaver fur made by an Athabaskan from Fort Yukon. In the mid-1800s, small glass beads became a popular trade currency for furs, and were valued as a colorful addition to porcupine quills, willow beads, seeds, animal hair, claws and beaks for embroidery on clothing. Beadwork designs today vary regionally. (Steve McCutcheon)

The one thing that has sustained through time is our dependence on animals for survival. Our lives follow the hunting seasons. In summertime, the Yukon River is lined with fish wheels and fish nets and people camping along the river, drying king salmon over racks. In fall, the Gwich'in people go out in their aluminum boats with outboard motors in search of moose and ducks, for winter food.

During the winter, after their wood supply is secure and previously obtained food has been stored, the Gwich'in snare rabbits, which they eat to supplement their diet of moose meat, dried fish, and ducks. Just as spring arrives, much to everyone's relief, the people rush to trap beaver and muskrats.

As children, my siblings and I used to squabble over the muskrat tails, which we would toast on the stove until they became crispy and were just like candy to us.

In time, Fort Yukon has adjusted to the many changes, good and bad. Today we have computers, fax machines, satellite dishes, cars, planes, telephones, cable television and much of everything else that the modern world has to offer. Yet we have remained simple in our values. The one thing that has held the Gwich'in people together through the chaos of change in the last 150 years is our deeply embedded relationship to the animals, land and subsistence lifestyle.

We are the Gwichyaa Gwich'in, "People of the Yukon Flats." □

Eyak

The smallest Native group in Alaska today is the Eyak. It is also the most recently recognized Native American group, a separate and distinct Indian culture. About 120 people living today are of Eyak descent.

Only one Eyak — Marie Smith Jones, the 78-year-old Chief — still speaks the language. Hers is a lonely distinction. "I sit in front of the TV. I talk and talk to it in my language, but it don't talk back. I pray in my language, but God don't talk back in it," said Jones, sitting at the kitchen table in her tiny Anchorage apartment. "When the pain gets so bad, then I call him. I call him just so I can hear my language again."

The "him" is Dr. Michael Krauss, a linguist at the Alaska Native Language Center in Fairbanks and the only other person in the world today who speaks Eyak. Krauss learned in the 1960s when he worked with Jones and Eyak Elders Anna Nelson Harry of Yakutat and Lena Saska Nacktan of Cordova to record Eyak stories and write an Eyak dictionary. Some of

Traditional
Homelands:

Eyak

the stories were published in 1982 as *In Honor of Eyak: the Art of Anna Nelson Harry.* Eyak is documented well enough to someday be revived as a spoken language, but for now Krauss calls it "a language of memory."

Meanwhile, an effort is underway to keep Eyak from becoming a culture of memory. A handful of Eyak descendants — including Jones' daughter Ramona Smith Curry and her great niece Jenna May, both in Anchorage, and Pam Smith, Glen "Dune" Lankard and Monica Reidel of Cordova — are learning

what it means to be Eyak, trying to revive their culture. "We are gaining visibility," asserts May. The Eyak and their friends are working to gain federal recognition for Eyak tribal status, regain ancestral lands in Cordova and support sobriety. With so much to do, learning the language is only a part. "We've accepted that we won't get the language fully recovered right now," said May, "but we are learning celebratory phrases to pass down."

FACING PAGE: *The bones of an unidentified Eyak man returned to Cordova by the Smithsonian Institution were repatriated on this spit, a former Eyak burial ground, in 1993. John F.C. Johnson (left), with the Chugach Heritage Foundation, arranged for return of the remains. He and Dune Lankard (right) prepare a burial spot under the guidance of Eyak Chief Marie Smith Jones (seated). (Photo courtesy of John F. C. Johnson)*

ABOVE: *Marie Smith Jones, the last Native Eyak speaker, sits in her Anchorage apartment on the eve of her 78th birthday. (L.J. Campbell, staff)*

ABOVE RIGHT: *Glen "Dune" Lankard speaks during the first Eyak potlatch in modern times, held in Cordova in June 1995. The seated dignitaries are, right to left, Maggie Escalita, an Athabaskan chief from Chitina; Marie Smith Jones, Eyak Chief; linguist Michael Krauss; and anthropologist Frederica de Laguna. Pam Smith, Dune's sister and an active Eyak revivalist in Cordova, is standing. (Soren Wuerth)*

Much of what is known about the Eyak comes from interviews and field work conducted by Frederica de Laguna and Kaj Birket-Smith, published as *The Eyak Indians of the Copper River Delta, Alaska* (1933). Krauss' work in the 1960s provided additional insights, in part through Anna Nelson Henry's masterful storytelling.

At the time of Russian arrival, the Eyaks occupied the Gulf of Alaska coast between present-day Cordova and Yakutat. According to old stories, the Eyak moved out of the Interior down the Copper River to the coast. Although Eyak has distant links to both Athabaskan and Tlingit, it started developing as a separate language about 3,500 years ago, according to Krauss.

On the coast, the Eyaks held rich salmon fishing grounds at the mouth of the Copper River. But they were a relatively small group, raided and squeezed by their neighbors, particularly the Chugach Alutiiq of Prince William Sound who claimed some of the same territory. The Eyak were friendlier with the Tlingits. Their social structures were similar, and intermarriages occurred frequently. But assimilation by the larger Tlingit society contributed to the disappearance of Eyak.

The Russians traded with the Eyak, sent them missionaries and recognized them as a distinct culture, even designating Eyak territory on their maps. But this was lost on the

Americans. By the 1880s, Tlingit expansion had pushed the remaining Eyaks into the Copper River delta, where about 200 Eyaks lived in two villages and several camps. The Americans arrived and started canneries, competing with the Eyaks for salmon. They introduced alcohol, disease and — from the Chinese cannery workers — opium. By 1900, the 60 surviving Eyaks had congregated at an old campsite near the canneries on the west end of Eyak Lake. In 1906, this last Eyak settlement, known as Old Town, became part of the new town of Cordova, created as a railroad port terminal.

Jones grew up in a two-room cabin on Eyak Lake with her sister and parents, Scar and Minnie Stevens, who worked for the railroad and salmon canneries. Although she was forbidden to speak her language at the government-run school in Cordova, she and her family conversed in Eyak at home. Her mother was devout Russian Orthodox, a faith Jones testifies to today, but raised her in Native ways. Her parents fished the salmon runs, taking her in the boat as a 4-day-old; they preserved berries in seal oil; her father showed her how to hunt and live off the land. She couldn't stomach milk as an infant; her mother chewed up fish and other foods to feed her. She remembers her mother getting help from a medicine woman once, and her parents told about Jones' maternal grandfather, a shaman, who used to go into a trance, balancing flat on a string strung across the living room. Jones started working in the canneries when she was 12, in 1930.

That's the year young Frederica de Laguna

landed in Cordova to begin anthropological work in Alaska. The U.S. Marshal directed de Laguna to the local Natives. De Laguna soon realized the Eyak language was unique and through her work, the Eyaks gained a place in the literature as the most recently re-recognized Alaska Native group. Jones remembers watching de Laguna and her associates interviewing "my favorite uncle. I pretended I was fishing on the beach, but I was watching them. I didn't want them to hurt him."

In the years that followed, de Laguna pioneered other documentation of Alaska's early Native people. Jones, meantime, stayed in Cordova through four marriages and a long bout with alcoholism. She quit drinking in 1970 and moved to Anchorage in 1973. In 1992, her sister Sophie died, leaving Jones as the last Native speaker of Eyak. She remembers calling Sophie to confer on the meaning of an elusive Eyak word, and together they'd remember.

Jones has emerged the past few years as something of an activist. She is outspoken against logging ancestral Eyak lands and participated in a lawsuit to stop clear-cutting by the Eyak Corp., a village corporation out of Cordova made up primarily of Chugach Alutiiqs and Tlingits. She is trying to fund a scholarship at the University of Alaska Fairbanks for Indian children. She feels that God has been preparing her to be the last speaker of the Eyak language. "I know I'm supposed to lead my people," she said.

As Eyak Chief, Jones has told her people's story at intertribal gatherings in the Lower 48 and carried the Eyak banner with her son, William, in the Alaska leg of the international Peace and Dignity Journey of indigenous people. Fliers from the events top the piles of papers in her apartment; the walls are covered with family photographs and Indian art. Jones has seven children — Leonard, Ramona and Sharon in Anchorage; William in Valdez; LaVina in Albuquerque; Sondra in Spokane; and JoAnna in Tucson — 25 grandchildren and 5 great-grandchildren.

In 1995, Jones and de Laguna returned together to Cordova for the first Eyak potlatch in 80 years. Dr. Krauss came also, greeting Jones in an outpouring of Eyak. The event was videotaped for a documentary, "More Than Words." The potlatch celebrated the reburial a year earlier of an unnamed Eyak man, whose bones had been held by the Smithsonian Institution since 1917. As Chief, Jones was to lead and she was nervous, afraid she would make a mistake. About two dozen people gathered in a mist at the burial site for a brief

healing ceremony, then adjourned to an empty warehouse for feasting, dancing and gift exchanges. Jones brought the celebration full circle by bestowing Eyak names to the young people. She chuckled at the name she chose for Lankard, an outspoken critic of logging Eyak lands. His Eyak name: *Jamachakih* means "little bird that never stops chirping." Said Jones, "He was a little chatterbox when he was young."

Later during the potlatch de Laguna commented: "It's a rebirth of a people.... The hope is in the children, who come to feel pride in being Eyak. We don't know the form Eyak culture will take in the future, but it will always be distinctly Eyak." ∎

Eyak descendants ceremoniously replanted trees on some of their ancestral grounds in Cordova that have been clear-cut by the Eyak Corp., a village corporation composed primarily of Alutiiqs and Tlingits of Cordova. (Jenna May)

Tlingit

The islands, seaways and rain forests of Southeast Alaska create a dramatic landscape, a place mysterious and awesome in scale and complexity. Jagged snow-capped peaks reach skyward, sometimes bathed by sunlight, often shrouded in fog and mist. Dense stands of cedar and spruce skirt the mountains in varying shades of gray, blue and green. The air resonates with the white noise of water cascading off the mountainsides, of streams seen and unseen coursing downhill into low-lying bogs and wetlands. Fjords gouged by ancient glaciers warp the coastline in a labyrinth of watery passages. Eagles and ravens soar overhead. Bear and wolf shadow the shore.

This is home to the Tlingit people, whose culture is as complex and dramatic as the land they inhabit.

Consider Tlingit art. Massive totem poles. Intricate weavings. Flamboyant headdresses. These and other visual expressions of the Tlingit culture are emblazoned with bold,

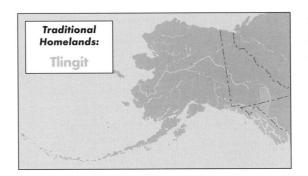

Traditional Homelands:
Tlingit

stylized designs that depict animals and humans. More than mere decorations, these designs are important crests. They signify ownership, relationships and family histories and are accompanied by stories that explain their origin, often connected with a legendary ancestor. Crests speak to a less visible but unifying — and complicated — aspect of Tlingit culture: Its social organization.

To start with, Tlingit society is divided into two parts, or moieties: Eagle and Raven. Relationships are traced through the mother's

family. A person is either Eagle or Raven, the same as his or her mother. Traditionally, marriages were between people of opposite moieties, but this practice isn't strictly observed today. The moieties are further divided into many families, or clans, each identified by their crests. Each moiety has more than a dozen different known clans today. Some of the Raven clans include Frog, Coho Salmon, Swan; those of the Eagle include Killer Whale, Shark and Bear, to name only a few. This determines how Tlingits are related to one another, past and present. Tlingits can follow their heritage

FACING PAGE: *This cedar clan house at Totem Bight State Historical Park, Ketchikan, is a replica of a Tlingit winter home. Traditionally, a clan house was built with hand-adzed planks and beams by the wife's relatives, who were repaid with a potlatch and gifts. (Francis Caldwell)*

LEFT: *Young Tlingit dancers from the Sitka Tribe pose in their regalia along the totem trail in the Sitka National Historical Park. (Francis Caldwell)*

ABOVE: *Tlingit weaver Marie Laws used narrow strips of sea otter fur in a Raven's Tail robe, shown here in progress in her house in Sitka. The technique, used by Tlingit weavers centuries ago, alternates wool and fur in the warp. The geometric design of the Raven's Tail appears as if woven completely in wool on one side; from the other side, the robe appears to be completely made of thick fur. She finished the robe in 1993 after more than 800 hours of work. (Photo courtesy of Sitka National Historical Park)*

through blood lines, home territories and ancestral clan houses. People in the same moiety may refer to each other as brothers and sisters, whether or not they are blood kin. In old Tlingit tradition, children were taught life skills by their maternal aunts and uncles.

"Basically, everyone is related in the community. We're all family, either through blood relations or through tribal ways," explains Mike Jackson, a Tlingit in Kake.

This has all sorts of implications: What one person does affects the entire community.

Younger people take care of the older people, who in turn teach them. If someone does something good or helps in some way, they are to be repaid with gifts or services of equal value. In the Tlingit way, people are taught to relate to each other with respect, rather than disrespect.

"My generation and the people who learned from Elders pass these things on to our children....We incorporate these values with Western style living. We walk on both sides," says Jackson, before turning back to business in the Kake village office. On this day, he is sorting through details of helping Kake establish a local tribal court, which will allow villagers to handle some problems of modern society through traditional Tlingit law. He also was thinking ahead to the weekend when a memorial potlatch for his late aunt would be held in the village. The opposite clan would host the event, as required by tradition. Jackson would conduct the services with words to remind people of their heritage.

"We shouldn't lose the values we are born with. We need to hold on to our identity. It makes a solid foundation to know who we are, to accept it, work with it and pass it on."

About 9,800 Tlingits live in Alaska today, most in Southeast's seaside towns and villages, such as Kake on Kupreanof Island. They are, by far, the largest Native group in Southeast. Tlingit ancestors may have lived on these same shores as long as 9,000 years ago, the age of the earliest known campsites; these early people probably depended on maritime resources and used boats, since their midden piles held bones of fish off the ocean bottom. Later sites, 4,000 and 3,000 years old, show more direct links with Tlingit-styled stone tools.

In the workshop of the Southeast Alaska Indian Cultural Center, carver Will Burkhart gives Camilla Gaine some advice on painting a red cedar hat to be worn during a pole-raising celebration in Sitka. Burkhart was head carver on a new totem raised in 1996; it was the first pole raised by the Sitka Tlingits since before the Russians took control. (Jim Lavrakas, Anchorage Daily News*)*

The temperate coastal environment of Southeast provided abundant resources, and Tlingit culture flourished. Prior to contact with outsiders and the diseases they brought, there may have been as many as 20,000 Tlingits living on the bays and inlets along Alaska's southeast coast, suggests Wallace M. Olson in *The Tlingit* (1991), a comprehensive introduction to Tlingit culture and history. Other important works about Tlingit culture include a series of books edited by Nora and Richard Dauenhauer with interviews, oral

histories, biographies and life stories collected from contemporary Tlingits, and writings by anthropologist Frederica de Laguna which draw from extensive field work in Tlingit country.

The early Tlingits repeatedly resisted intrusions into their territory. They battled the Russians numerous times at different locations, including Yakutat and Sitka. Their practice of exacting retribution for trespass and wrong-doing resulted in tragic confrontation after Alaska became a U.S. territory; when the people of Angoon demanded payment for the

A totem park in Klawock, on Prince of Wales Island, holds restored and replicated totems from the old Tlingit village of Tuxekan. Most of the 800 people in Klawock are Tlingit. (Don Pitcher)

lives of two villagers killed in an explosion at a nearby cannery, the Navy sent in a warship and destroyed the village. At the turn of the century, the Tlingits were squeezed off their traditional fishing, hunting and village sites by American gold miners, cannery operators and the federal government's new Tongass National Forest. Tlingit leaders decided in 1912 that the clans needed to unite to claim their rights, and formed the Alaska Native Brotherhood and, several years later, the Alaska Native Sisterhood. With passage in 1924 of the citizenship act for Indians and Eskimos, Tlingits increased their political force. Tlingit William Paul was elected to the Territorial Legislature that year, the first Alaska Native to be elected. In the mid-1930s, the Tlingits joined with the Haidas to press the first Native land claims lawsuit in Alaska against the federal government.

The Tlingit sense of ownership remains strong; they value the ethic of fairness. Dances, songs, stories and clan crests are "owned" by individuals and clans. A source of irritation among some Tlingits today is what they see as disrespect from visitors who take pictures, make tape recordings or copy crest designs without permission.

The Tlingit are well-recognized for many remarkable visual expressions of their culture. They are noted woodworkers and weavers. They historically built huge clan houses out of

ABOVE: *This detail is from the Eagle totem pole in front of Chief Shakes House on Shakes Island, Wrangell, home to the Stikine Tlingits. (Don Pitcher)*

ABOVE RIGHT: *On Christmas Day, the people of Angoon on Admiralty Island gather at the Alaska Native Brotherhood Hall for the "community tree" gift exchange. Bessie and Matthew Fred, Chief of the Raven clan and a community leader, accept their gifts. (Don Pitcher)*

cedar planks for their winter villages; sleeping areas inside were screened off with elaborately carved panels; similar clan houses today are built for community gatherings. They also carved great ocean-going canoes from huge logs. They carved totem poles to tell stories and histories; the carver would be commissioned by a member of the opposite moiety. Totem poles are still carved today. When the completed pole is raised, the carver tells what the designs signify, the story of the pole. The pole's owner pays the carver and all those who helped, often by hosting a potlatch party. Today weaving continues, although not to the degree of past centuries when most clothing, baskets and other practical and ceremonial items were woven from cedar bark, wool, roots and strips of fur. Often at potlatches in the past, robes that might have taken months or years to weave would be snipped apart and given away in a show of wealth. A dedicated group of weavers is hard at work in Southeast today to keep the art going. They are working individually and in collaboration to rebuild a cultural inventory. They have completed several large pieces of ceremonial regalia, such as Chilkat and Raven's Tail robes, that are brought out for special

LEFT: *Richard Reese and David Ramos dig for cockles on Khantaak Island near Yakutat. Gathering beach foods, such as cockles, clams, chitons and kelp, is a widespread subsistence activity practiced by Tlingits and other Natives in Southeast, as well as elsewhere along Alaska's coast. (Karen Jetmar)*

BELOW LEFT: *Ray Smith performs with the Tlingit-Haida Dancers of Anchorage. "We're so far removed from our homes," said Linda Dewitt, of Wrangell, who helped start the group in 1986 so Tlingit and Haida people in Anchorage could learn songs from their culture. Today as many as 50 dancers, mostly Tlingits, participate. (Danny Daniels)*

occasions such as Celebration, a festival held in Juneau in even-numbered years. Traditionally, only men carved and women wove, but now a few women are carving and a few men are learning to weave.

The Tlingits share cultural similarities with the Haida and Tsimshian, but the languages are all different. The Tlingits share definite linguistic similarities in verb structures to the Athabaskans and so the two were linked long ago at some point in the NaDene Indian migration. Tlingit stories tell of how the people came to the coast, some under a glacier, from the Interior. A group of Tlingits moved to inland Canada from the coast during early contact with traders.

Few people younger than 45 are fluent in Tlingit today, although there are numerous attempts to rekindle use of the language. As in Alaska's other Native cultures, many things important to the culture have no equivalent in English, so maintaining the language is seen by many as vital to maintaining the culture. Village schools offer Tlingit language classes, and one school in Juneau offers a Tlingit immersion program.

In Sitka, Pauline Duncan has developed her own approach. She teaches Tlingit to her first-graders by using Tlingit words throughout the day. Classroom rules are given in Tlingit, the children exchange greetings in the morning and afternoon in Tlingit. When they study rocks and minerals or insects, they learn the names in Tlingit as well as English. They even say the pledge to the flag in Tlingit. Although Pauline is Tlingit and heard the language as a child in Angoon, she never learned to speak it because she was away at boarding school. She started teaching Tlingit in her class several years ago, partly as a way to learn. Her husband Albert, a fluent speaker who grew up in a fish camp on Excursion Inlet, helps her with vocabulary and grammar. She also visits regularly with Tlingit Elders in Sitka. Along with the language, she teaches about other aspects of the culture, bringing in Native foods for the kids to try and inviting Elders in to tell stories. Even the children in her class who come from other cultural backgrounds benefit, she says. "The Tlingit culture is of this area, a part of the history. It's building a foundation so they can extend what they're learning about the Tlingits to cultures they may encounter later in life. They'll know that wherever they live, there is a local culture, with language, dance, customs and stories." ■

Carving Traditions

By Nathan Jackson

Editor's note: *Tlingit carver Nathan Jackson shared these thoughts with his wife Dorica, who transcribed them during a hectic month, which included finishing and launching a 28-foot traditional cedar dugout canoe in Saxman while concurrently working on a 35-foot totem pole for Totem Bight State Park in Ketchikan. The Jacksons live south of Saxman; they choose not to have a television in their home, and they heat by wood. Son Stephen attends college in Idaho; in 1995 he carved a totem pole under his father's supervision for the Veteran's Administration homeless shelter in Anchorage. Daughter Rebecca graduated from high school in May 1996. Jackson's work can be seen around the world and throughout Alaska, including at the University of Alaska Museum in Fairbanks, the Anchorage Museum of History and Art and the Alaska State Museum in Juneau. In 1995, he was designated a "living cultural treasure" with a National Heritage Fellowship from the National Endowment for the Arts. He also is pictured in his Raven regalia on a new U.S. postage stamp, part of a set featuring American Indian dances released in 1996.*

As a young person, I was asked to practice Native dancing for the Fourth of July. We spent some time with all the Elders, learning some songs and how to dance. I did not take that much interest in it, because it took me away from my buddies. But then I found out that my buddies weren't doing anything that exciting anyway. So I danced on a flatbed truck in the Fourth of July parade. My grandfather felt it would be better for me to try to learn the old ways, and my feeling was that at the time I wanted to learn the easier way.

During the winter months as a teenager, I spent a lot of time cutting wood and watching my uncle, Ted Laurence, carve small totem poles. He asked me to try a small totem pole about four inches high. It wasn't too bad, but I didn't think that I wanted to continue carving. Since my grandfather was teaching me how to fish, I wanted to be a fisherman.

After serving in the Army, I came back to Southeast where I fished and looked for odd jobs, which wasn't too successful. In 1962, I ended up in the hospital at Mt. Edgecumbe in Sitka because they thought I had tuberculosis. Through occupational therapy, a lot of yellow cedar was available, so I filled up the whole showcase with small poles. After a couple of months I was released, and I ended up dancing with the Chilkat Dancers in Haines. Some carvers in Haines were working at Alaska Indian Arts Inc., and there I met Leo Jacobs, who did miniature poles. I also had another uncle, Horace Marks, who had carved.

Nathan Jackson works on a cedar Raven mask at the Saxman Tribal House. (Hall Anderson)

I felt that I could be able to make a living at carving, rather than trying to be a fisherman.

During this time, I also took an interest in doing portraits. That fall, I was accepted to the Institute of American Indian Arts in Santa Fe, New Mexico, where I spent two years. Then the opportunity came to go with Alaska Indian Arts to the 1964 World's Fair in New York. It gave me an opportunity to look at and study some of the Tlingit art at the various museums in New York. Later, back in Haines, I worked as an instructor for Alaska Indian Arts. I met Bill Holm, an authority on Northwest Coast Indian Art from Seattle, who pointed out a lot of elements in flat design during a class he was teaching in Haines. It enlightened my understanding of two-dimensional Native design. I inquired from Bill, on the side, about the adzing techniques used on the old poles and spent a lot of time practicing and making my own tools. From Bill, I have gotten a lot of referrals for jobs, which helped launch my career.

I spent much time looking at art pieces in museums and studying those pieces. Drawing, at least for me, is pretty important to come up with a likeness of any art pieces. You have to be able to see what

Nathan Jackson touches up the paint on Kitch-xan *(Thundering Eagle), which stands in downtown Ketchikan. (Hall Anderson)*

you are looking at, and you have to be able to critique your own work. In totem pole work, at least in Southeast Alaska, there are three different styles — Tsimshian, Haida, and Tlingit — so you have to be able to distinguish the difference and try not to overlap. The Haidas used large red cedar, bigger in diameter than the Tsimshian and Tlingit poles. The eyes on each figure were fairly large, and there was a lot of interconnecting with the various figures. The Tsimshian

from the upper Skeena River, in British Columbia, used longer trees. Tsimshian figures are more rounded and realistic than the Haida, and the eyes are not as large in proportion to the face. The Tlingit style is closer to the Tsimshian than the Haida, with rounded-off figures and fairly deep carving. The main difference between the Tlingit and the Tsimshian is the treatment of the face. In doing reproductions, I've had to do the Haida style, and in doing research I've made a lot of interesting discoveries.

In my original work, I basically try to maintain the traditional Tlingit style in such things as masks, totem poles, etc. There have been a few exceptions, such as an eagle in Ketchikan called Thundering Wings. In our language, this is called *Kitch-xan: Kitch* meaning "wings," and *xan* meaning "sound of thunder." This piece is a fairly realistic representation of an eagle, with Tlingit elements in the wing designs, tail and treatment of the head. The only completely nontraditional carving I have done was two sets of doors, carved in low relief, for a church in Ketchikan. The subject matter was from the Hebrew scriptures.

I enjoy doing artwork that has been commissioned by my own people, such as the headdresses and masks, because they won't be sitting on a wall but they'll be used. It probably means more to me to be recognized by my people. I have been commissioned to do both woodcarving and jewelry. Generally I prefer working on bigger projects, such as totem poles, large screens and canoes.

Stephen Jackson (left) helps his dad tend steaming water inside a 28-foot cedar canoe which Nathan carved in 1995. In four hours of steaming, the sides of the dugout canoe spread apart from 36 inches to 54 inches. "It opened up like a flower," recalls Dorica Jackson. The water was boiled by continually dropping in hot ingots, heated atop wood-burning barrel furnaces. Plastic covers helped regulate the steaming. The canoe was later painted with Eagle and Raven crests on the bow and stern and successfully launched. It now resides in Saxman. (Hall Anderson)

Over the years, I have had jobs that required, in the contract, that I take apprentices. I also have had people ask to apprentice with me. And then, there's my son Stephen, probably my best apprentice yet. A prerequisite for an apprentice is desire to learn to carve, a little drawing ability, and possibly artists in the family background. I get them started on making or buying their own tools. At one time after I came to Ketchikan, someone referred to me as "Nathan Jackson,

the last of the Tlingit carvers." I had a pretty negative reaction to this because I felt there were many more carvers on the horizon, given the opportunity. This is one reason why I took them on. Eventually, most apprentices launch off on their own and develop their own styles. Many of them have been fairly successful in making a living from carving.

One of the misconceptions that some people have about the art is that totem poles were worshipped.

That's not true. In the olden days, the poles would reflect different stories relating to a particular clan. Since there was no written language, it was a way to remind the Elders to tell the young people about their heritage by what the totem poles meant. Some were stories of heroism and morals, and then some were about unpaid debts. Usually the tallest poles would show rank and nobility, and so in the olden days when a canoe full of people would come to a village, they would know which house to go to first.

Sometimes I kind of feel like a trailblazer who has looked over an old trail covered with brush that needed to be cleared away, so the trail could be re-established. Through digging and looking at old works, I wonder what a lot of the old-time master carvers went through and how they were dedicated to their work. I appreciate being able to try to copy, or reproduce, some of the older works. I feel fortunate that I have been able to receive large commissions and make a living as an artist, and that I have been able to watch others follow and also be successful. I can see a lot of good carvers on the horizon, and this makes me want to forge ahead, to continue to improve. □

Tsimshian

For four days they feasted. The Raven clan presented salmon on the first day. The Killer Whale clan served halibut the second. The Wolf clan prepared deer for the third. And on the fourth day, the Eagle clan hosted with every traditional Tsimshian food imaginable — fish eggs, hooligan, seaweed, clams, cockles, abalone, crab, fry bread, blueberries, salmonberries, "half-dried" fish that had been smoked over alder then steamed. For four days the Tsimshian Indians of Metlakatla and their guests feasted, danced, sang and celebrated the raising of three newly carved totem poles. "It was the neatest thing that ever happened," recalls Metlakatla resident Theo McIntyre.

For nearly 100 years, the Tsimshians of Metlakatla on Annette Island in Southeast Alaska were separated from the most visible of their Indian traditions — carving, singing, dancing and potlatching. The founders of Metlakatla had chosen to adopt the "white man's ways," the people say, when they left their

Traditional Homelands: Tsimshian

Tsimshian villages in British Columbia to join Anglican preacher William Duncan. Missionary Duncan enticed a group of Tsimshians to create with him a "model" community, to escape the damaging influences of alcohol and disease brought by visitors on steamships through Canada. About 800 Tsimshians followed Duncan to Alaska in 1887, 90 miles north to the site of an abandoned Tlingit village on Annette Island. Here they built the new town of Metlakatla. Duncan obtained the 86,000-acre island from the U.S. government as a reser-

vation before he died. Today the Tsimshians of Metlakatla live on the only federally recognized Indian reservation in Alaska.

"We almost completely adopted the culture of the white man, and we've done real good with it. Now we're just getting back into our own," says Tsimshian artist and knife-maker Jack Hudson, who teaches traditional carving at the school. Hudson reintroduced carving to the Metlakatla Tsimshians in 1974, when he came home for a visit and ended up staying. He had been living at the time in Washington state, studying old Tsimshian works in museums and carving under the tutelage of Northwest Coast Indian Art expert Bill Holm. In 1996, Hudson

FACING PAGE: *In 1994, the Tsimshians of Metlakatla held a four-day potlatch to celebrate raising new totem poles. Here they are gathered at the senior center to dedicate the new poles. (Hall Anderson)*

LEFT: *In 1996, artist Wayne Hewson painted Tsimshian designs on the waterfront side of the community's longhouse. Hewson's design incorporates each crest of Metlakatla's four clans. In strict tradition, only one clan crest would be used, but combining clan crests to show unity is an emerging tradition throughout Southeast Native communities. (Hall Anderson)*

LOWER LEFT: *Miquel'l Askren, 14, a member of Metlakatla's Fourth Generation Dancers, wears an Eagle headpiece made of cedar and abalone. Her apron features "hands of friendship" with her Eagle crest in the center. Her Tsimshian name,* Shgu'Goad Lax Shgeet, *means "Devoted Eagle." She has been dancing since she was 3. (Hall Anderson)*

was in his 22nd year at the Metlakatla high school where he teaches about 60 students a year aspects of traditional Tsimshian art. When the students complete his program, they can create and connect the seven elements of Tsimshian design into human and animal figures in drawing, painting and carving. Each student also makes eight carving knives and an adze, tools crucial to the art. The knife metal comes from old bandsaws from the community's sawmill; the adzes are made from old car springs. Hudson, an internationally recognized artist, figures each student comes out of the program with a personally tailored set of too!s worth about $500.

About the same time carving returned to Metlakatla, so did dancing. In the 1970s, several local people visited the Tsimshians in British Columbia to learn songs and movements to teach Metlakatla's school children as part of the federally funded Johnson O'Malley Indian Education program. The school program was so successful that parents of those dancing youths started the community group Fourth Generation Dancers, taking their name from being fourth generation descendants of the town's founders. Several people, including David Boxley, Barbara Fawcett and Melody Leask, wrote many of the songs that the group performs today. "Our Song" tells the history of Metlakatla. Another dance called "*Whywah,*" a Tsimshian word meaning "Let's go!," came from Metlakatla crowds yelling "*whywah*" at basketball games; the song is used to invite audience members to dance. The group also performs "Eagle, Drop Me a Feather," written by McIntrye's daughter, Marcella, when she was 12. She was inspired by seeing her mother walking the beach, looking for eagle feathers and thanking the eagle when she found one. In this dance, Eagle clan members dance in the center with feathers, calling "*shkeek*" (eagle) to the sky. In the course of the dance, they drop their feathers to dancers in the outer circle who say "*gom golth wan,*" or thank you.

"It's living proof that we're making a difference with our young people. It gives them more pride in who they are," asserts McIntyre. "When I was growing up, I went to Indian boarding school in Lawrence, Kansas. The young people there would put on their traditional regalia and dance. For the few of us from Metlakatla, we wished we had something like that...well, now I have and it will be handed down to my children, my grandchildren." In August 1997, the dancers plan a reunion potlatch to celebrate the group's 10-year anniversary.

"Our great grandfathers were raised through the church," McIntrye continues. "None of the traditional carvings or the dancing was done here. We're not blaming," she adds. "He (Duncan) did good. We're very proud of this community."

Modern Metlakatla has a sawmill and salmon cannery and several small businesses including a meat market, grocery, hardware store and hotel.

About 1,500 members of the Metlakatla Indian community live on the island today. The community regulates who can live and work there, requiring permits and local sponsors for outsiders who want to stay any length of time. People still worship in the faith that Duncan brought, although the town now has churches of four other denominations. Although Duncan appreciated Tsimshian art — he had four totem poles inside his original church in B.C. — he encouraged the people to use their time in more economically productive ways, and artistic expressions withered among Metlakatlans. He did, however, learn and encourage use of the language, which apparently thrived until the government school teachers arrived in the early 1900s with their English-only mandate. Today, Tsimshian is taught in the Metlakatla schools and classes are held in the evenings for adults. McIntyre estimates that a quarter of the residents, mostly people over age 40, speak Tsimshian conversationally; linguists at the Alaska Native Language Center in Fairbanks put the number of fluent Tsimshian speakers at a fraction of that.

Fishing, hunting and gathering beach foods today remain the strongest link to ancestral Tsimshian ways. The local store brings convenience, but nothing replaces the locally harvested foods found in every freezer and cupboard. Tiny little buildings all around town are smokehouses used to dry fish and seaweeds. In addition to seafoods and edible plants and berries, people hunt deer which live on the island. Wayne Hewson, a well-known Tsimshian artist and carver, likes to eat deer and also uses the hooves for making dance

rattles. His freezer is crammed with deer legs dropped off by friends after hunting trips.

In 1996, Hewson took on a major art project — painting Tsimshian designs on the community longhouse, part of a larger effort to get Metlakatla ready for tourists. The community voted to tap into Southeast's lucrative visitor industry by offering tour packages to cruise ship passengers, selling the tours from a booth in the Ketchikan visitor's center. Ketchikan is about 15 minutes by air north of Metlakatla; an hour by state ferry. Metlakatla usually gets a few hundred visitors each summer, mostly independent travelers who come by ferry. By tapping cruise ships, the community expects to host perhaps as many as 6,000 people a summer. Guests tour the town, including Duncan's cottage and museum, the original church and the historic 1918 cannery, then stop at the longhouse for pit-baked salmon, traditional dancing and visits with Tsimshian artists. Metlakatla flirted with tourism in the mid-1980s, when an outside company hired locals to drive buses and cook salmon for visitors. But this time, the Metlakatla Indian Community is in charge

and with recent downturns in the salmon industry, most townspeople seem ready for a new economy, eager to share their recovered Tsimshian traditions. ∎

TOP RIGHT: *This detail is from David Boxley's memorial pole to his grandfather Albert Bolton, who died at age 98 in 1992. Boxley has carved 11 of Metlakatla's 13 poles. (Hall Anderson)*

RIGHT: *Metlakatlans carry a 32-foot red cedar pole carved by David Boxley to the senior center where it will be pulled to standing with ropes. (Hall Anderson)*

Haida

Today in Alaska, the Haida Indians are often linked to the Tlingit. The Tlingit-Haida Central Council oversees Native land allotments in Southeast; the Tlingit-Haida Housing Authority handles government-funded housing projects; the Tlingit-Haida Dancers of Anchorage perform traditional songs and ceremonies in the state's largest Native village. The Haida and the Tlingit, along with the Tsimshian, do share cultural similarities with each other, as well as with several other groups of indigenous people in the temperate rain forests along the northwest Pacific coast: They express themselves artistically through carving, painting and weaving in a style categorically referred to as Northwest Coast Indian Art, and their societies are traditionally structured around complex relationships defined by kinships through their mothers' families.

But the Haida are a distinct and separate group of people, with their own language. Some people think the Haida language may

Traditional Homelands:

Haida

stem from the same source as Tlingit, Eyak and Athabaskan. Linguists at the Alaska Native Language Center in Fairbanks, however, see no connections between Haida and other known languages; they consider the Haida language an "isolate." This makes the Haida's ancient origins something of a mystery.

In more recent times, the Haidas came to Alaska from Canada. Today about 1,100 Haidas live in the state, with most concentrated in southern Southeast. Hydaburg, a quiet village at the end of a gravel road south of

Craig on Prince of Wales Island, is the primary Haida community in Alaska, although Klawock, Craig and Ketchikan have sizable Haida populations. British Columbia remains the Haida cultural center, with a large community in Masset, on Graham Island. Visiting regularly takes place between the Alaskan and Canadian Haidas.

Mona Frank Jackson, 83, a Haida living today in Kake, remembers her early childhood in Masset where she lived with her grandparents in a clan house. The clan house was "one big room, like a warehouse," she recalls. She slept with her grandparents on a big featherbed surrounded by "copperhead trunks." Her grandfather got up first every morning to

FACING PAGE: *Totems from abandoned Haida villages on southern Prince of Wales Island stand today in Hydaburg, a quiet village of about 500 people. (Don Pitcher)*

Two Haida canoes (36-foot Seal Hunter *in lead and 42-foot* Eagle Beak *in rear) approach Saxman for a Haida family reunion. The canoes were paddled 90 miles from Masset, B.C. As the canoeists near Saxman, the* Sky Princess *cruise ship heads out after a day in Ketchikan. (Hall Anderson)*

make coffee on a big wood stove. Three uncles also lived in the house. One made boats in the community's big boat house; another was an accomplished piano player; the third was a reader in the Episcopal church. The family would pick berries, fish and garden.

She moved to Hydaburg in 1923 at age 10 to join her mother who had remarried. It was a difficult adjustment. She was timid and scared of white people and she spoke no English,

which was the only language allowed in the Hydaburg school. In the fourth grade, she was sent to the Sheldon Jackson boarding school in Sitka. She made infrequent visits to Hydaburg to see her mother. On one visit home, the family, including her grandmother, traveled in a traditional dugout canoe to Kake for a potlatch. As they beached the canoe, her grandmother pointed to a young man on the beach. "That's the man you'll marry," she said. Later as a school teacher, Jackson took her first job in Kake. The school board president who met her at the steamship was Thomas Jackson, the boy from the beach; true to her grandmother's prediction, they married.

But long before this story took place, the first Haidas came to Alaska.

The Haida's aboriginal homeland is the Queen Charlotte Islands, an archipelago of two

large islands and 150 smaller ones. Sometime in the 1700s, a group of Haida from the storm-lashed shore of Graham Island, largest of the Queen Charlottes, abandoned their villages and came to Alaska. They paddled their long, graceful cedar canoes across 30 miles of ocean to Prince of Wales, Dall, Long and Sukkwan islands in Southeast.

The Haidas in Alaska, often called "Kaigani" after an early village, named themselves *Kiis Haade*, the "separate island people." They chose winter village sites on protected waters with sloping shores for landing their canoes. The Alaska rain forests were similar, but lacked cedar trees as massive and tall as those they left behind. They had access to most of the same seafood and sea mammals, including halibut, cod, seals, sea lions, sea otters, mussels, clams, crabs and octopus. The new territory also had deer, wolf, mink and beaver, animals absent in their southerly homeland.

They kept track of the year by seasonal activity. For instance, *Qong qons*, or Great Month (June) brought canoe loads of Haida singing ceremonial songs to bird rookeries to gather eggs; some were preserved in eulachon grease for winter. Grease from eulachon, smeltlike fish, came in trade from Tsimshian on the B.C. mainland and was highly valued as a preservative, flavoring and delicacy. During *San gias*, the Killer Whale Month (July) women and children hiked into the mountains to gather cedar bark; the ripping of the bark from the tree was likened to a killer whale blowing. The Haida built cedar plank houses where their extended families lived, and they carved totem poles to tell family histories, myths and to hold the remains of the dead. To commission a house building or totem carving required payment for services with elaborate potlatches.

When Spaniard Juan Perez sighted the Queen Charlottes in 1774, the Haida were already well-established in Alaska. Englishman George Dixon first traded sea otter pelts with the Haida in 1787, triggering a steady summer fleet of fur traders. The Haida, they noted, had an elaborate and sophisticated material culture; they prized iron in trade to make adzes, which increased their carving efficiency. The Haida also started producing carvings from argillite, a black shale, and spruce root baskets and hats for trade souvenirs.

By the late 1800s, the Haida adopted Christianity. They'd mostly replaced their cedar-bark and skin clothing with western dress. By this time, the Alaska Haidas had five permanent winter villages: Koiandlas and Howkan on Long Island; Sukkwan on Sukkwan Island; and Klinkwan and Kasaan on Prince of Wales. In 1884, with passage of the Organic Act and establishment of civil government in Alaska, Howkan and Klinkwan got government schools. By 1900, modern two-story houses started appearing on ruins of the communal houses in Howkan and Klinkwan. Totem poles cut down in Klinkwan appeared as supports for a new boardwalk built along the beachfront. In 1902, the people of Kasaan were promised jobs if they moved to the site of a new copper mine at New Kasaan, where they lived until the operation closed, then moved to Ketchikan in the 1940s and 1950s. In 1912, many people from the other villages moved to a new village,

Hydaburg, to get a new government school.

Clara Natkong, 87, moved to Hydaburg as a 3-year-old with her family from Howkan. She remembers her father, who was raised by his mother's brother in the traditional way, telling stories and teaching songs. Today, Natkong tells the stories to Hydaburg children. "An important part of passing on our culture is

BELOW: *The carved "seal rock" petroglyph from the old village of Howkan can be seen today in Hydaburg, the main Haida community in Alaska. (Sharon Brosamle)*

RIGHT: *This replica of a housepost from the old village of Howkan shows interconnected figures, one of the distinguishing characteristics of Haida totem carving. This post stands in Hydaburg. (Sharon Brosamle)*

telling stories. We have many, many stories, all kinds of stories. Hearing them is how I remember them." Starting in the 1970s, she taught Haida language in the school; a Haida language and culture program continues in the school today. But now the children come to Natkong's house for stories, so she doesn't have to walk up the hill to the school. "Quite a few here can talk in Haida," she says. "It's not a forgotten language. Yesterday I was out riding with my grandchildren and they were saying things in Haida. It's really nice." ∎

Delores Churchill: Master Weaver

Well-known Haida weaver Delores Churchill (left) holds a Chilkat robe of intricate design, which took her a year to complete. Daughter Holly holds a shaman's apron she made with cedar bark. (Hall Anderson)

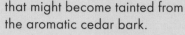

Delores Churchill, 66, learned weaving from her mother Selina Peratrovich, whose weavings were highly prized by collectors. Mrs. Peratrovich wove and taught until her death in 1984 at age 95. "If it wasn't for her the art of (Haida) basketry would have died. No one was teaching it," said Churchill.

Churchill started weaving at age 42. When she walked into her mother's class for her first lesson, her mother looked up and said, "What you do here? I weave, I weave. You no look. You go home." But Churchill stayed. "She made me take my basket undone over and over," she recalls. "I didn't think I was any good." Not until several years later did she learn how her mother bragged on her abilities to other people.

Churchill also knows weaving techniques from other Native cultures, taught to her by their master weavers. One distinction is the direction of the weave: Tsimshians and Tlingits weave rightside up; Haidas and Aleuts weave upside down. Cedar bark and spruce roots are commonly used materials. Spruce roots are used in baskets to carry delicate foods, such as berries and clams, that might become tainted from the aromatic cedar bark.

Churchill enjoys gathering bark and roots; the forest is like a cathedral, she says. Done correctly, stripping the bark or pulling feeder roots in the spring won't harm the tree. "When we get the roots, we cover the ground back up with moss, so there's no chance of the tree being unearthed by erosion. I like to teach (students) to respect all living things...to be cognizant that we're the intruders."

"One thing my mother always did was to thank the trees, and I find myself doing it in my old age, telling the tree that I'm going to make a beautiful basket and hope it has a long life. Whenever I go out and climb the mountains now, I think of her." □

Today, Churchill weaves elaborate Haida regalia, baskets and hats, mostly on commission. She stays busy teaching around the state, as in this spruce-root weaving workshop in Kodiak, and studies old Haida weavings in museums around the world. (Joe Kelley)

Bibliography

Alaska Native Knowledge Network [on-line], April 1996. Available: http://zorba.uafadm.alaska.edu/ankn/index.html

Bergsland, Knut and Moses Dirks, Eds. *Unangam Ungiikangin Kayux Tunusangin • Unangam Uniikangis Ama Tunuzangis • Aleut Tales and Narratives.* Collected 1909-1910 by Waldemar Jochelson. Fairbanks: Alaska Native Language Center, University of Alaska, 1990.

Blackman, Margaret B. *Window on the Past: The Photographic Ethnohistory of the Northern and Kaigani Haida.* Ottawa, National Museum of Canada, 1981.

Chaussonnet, Valérie. *Crossroads Alaska, Native Cultures of Alaska and Siberia.* Washington, D.C.: Arctic Studies Center, Smithsonian Institution, 1995.

Dauenhauer, Nora Marks and Richard Dauenhauer, Eds. *Haa Kisteeyí, Our Culture, Tlingit Life Stories.* Juneau and Seattle: Sealaska Heritage Foundation and University of Washington Press, 1994.

Fienup-Riordan, Ann. *The Living Tradition of Yup'ik Masks.* Seattle: University of Washington Press, 1996.

_____ Ed. *Agayuliyararput, Our Way of Making Prayer, Yup'ik Masks and the Stories They Tell.* Transcribed and translated by Marie Meade. Anchorage: Anchorage Museum of History and Art, 1996.

Fogel-Chance, Nancy. "Living in Both Worlds: Inupiaq Women and Urban Life," *Arctic Circle* [on-line], March 1996. Available: http://www.lib.uconn.edu/ArcticCircle/CulturalViability/Inupiat/nfc1.html

Halliday, Jan and Gail Chehak. *Native Peoples of the Northwest.* Seattle: Sasquatch Books, 1996.

Damas, David, Ed. *Handbook of North American Indians, Vol. 5, Arctic.* Washington, D.C.: Smithsonian Institution, 1984.

Irwin, Mike, Ed. *Alaska Natives Commission Final Report.* Vols. I, II and III. Anchorage: Alaska Natives Commission, Joint Federal-State Commission on Policies and Programs Affecting Alaska Natives, 1994.

Johnson, John F.C., Ed. *Chugach Legends, Stories and Photographs of the Chugach Region.* Anchorage: Chugach Alaska Corp., 1984.

Kawagley, A. Oscar. *A Yupiaq Worldview, A Pathway to Ecology and Spirit.* Prospect Heights, IL: Waveland Press Inc., 1995.

Krauss, Michael E., Ed. *In Honor of Eyak, The Art of Anna Nelson Harry.* Fairbanks: Alaska Native Language Center, University of Alaska, 1982.

Langdon, Steve J. *The Native People of Alaska.* Anchorage: Greatland Graphics, 1987.

Olson, Wallace M. *The Tlingit, An Introduction to their Culture and History.* Auke Bay, AK: Heritage Research, 1991.

Many other *ALASKA GEOGRAPHIC®* issues provide additional information about Alaska Natives and their homeland regions, including:
Alaska Native Arts and Crafts, Vol. 12, No. 3
Alaska's Native People, Vol. 6, No. 3
Alaska's Seward Peninsula, Vol. 14, No. 3
The Aleutian Islands, Vol. 22, No. 2
Kodiak Island, Vol. 19, No. 3
The Kotzebue Basin, Vol 8, No. 3
The Lower Yukon River, Vol. 17, No. 4
The Middle Yukon River, Vol. 17, No. 3
North Slope Now, Vol. 16, No. 2
The Nushagak River, Vol. 17, No. 1
Southeast Alaska, Vol. 20, No. 2 ☐

Index

ALASKA GEOGRAPHIC. Back Issues

Membership in The Alaska Geographic Society includes a subscription to *ALASKA GEOGRAPHIC*®, the Society's colorful, award-winning quarterly. Contact us for current membership rates or to request a copy of our free catalog.

The *ALASKA GEOGRAPHIC*® back issues listed below can be ordered directly from us. **NOTE:** This list was current in mid 2003. If more than a year has elapsed since that time, please contact us before ordering to check prices and availability of back issues, particularly those marked "Limited."

When ordering back issues please add $5 for the first book and $2 for each additional book ordered to cover shipping and handling. Inquire for shipping rates to non-U.S. addresses. To order, send check or money order (U.S. funds) or VISA or MasterCard information (including expiration date and daytime phone number) with list of titles desired to:

ALASKA GEOGRAPHIC.
P.O. Box 93370 • Anchorage, AK 99509-3370
Phone (907) 562-0164 • Toll free (888) 255-6697
Fax (907) 562-0479 • e-mail: info@akgeo.com
Web: www.akgeo.com

The North Slope, Vol. 1, No. 1. Out of print.
One Man's Wilderness, Vol. 1, No. 2. Out of print.
Admiralty...Island in Contention, Vol. 1, No. 3. $9.95.
Fisheries of the North Pacific, Vol. 1, No. 4. Out of print.
Alaska-Yukon Wild Flowers, Vol. 2, No. 1. Out of print.
Richard Harrington's Yukon, Vol. 2, No. 2. Out of print.
Prince William Sound, Vol. 2, No. 3. Out of print.
Yakutat: The Turbulent Crescent, Vol. 2, No. 4. Out of print.
Glacier Bay: Old Ice, New Land, Vol. 3, No. 1. Out of print.
The Land: Eye of the Storm, Vol. 3, No. 2. Out of print.
Richard Harrington's Antarctic, Vol. 3, No. 3. $9.95.
The Silver Years, Vol. 3, No. 4. $24.95. Limited.
Alaska's Volcanoes, Vol. 4, No. 1. Out of print.
The Brooks Range, Vol. 4, No. 2. Out of print.
Kodiak: Island of Change, Vol. 4, No. 3. Out of print.
Wilderness Proposals, Vol. 4, No. 4. Out of print.
Cook Inlet Country, Vol. 5, No. 1. Out of print.
Southeast: Alaska's Panhandle, Vol. 5, No. 2. Out of print.
Bristol Bay Basin, Vol. 5, No. 3. Out of print.
Alaska Whales and Whaling, Vol. 5, No. 4. $19.95.
Yukon-Kuskokwim Delta, Vol. 6, No. 1. Out of print.
Aurora Borealis, Vol. 6, No. 2. $24.95. Limited
Alaska's Native People, Vol. 6, No. 3. $29.95. Limited.
The Stikine River, Vol. 6, No. 4. $9.95.
Alaska's Great Interior, Vol. 7, No. 1. $19.95.

Photographic Geography of Alaska, Vol. 7, No. 2. Out of print.
The Aleutians, Vol. 7, No. 3. Out of print.
Klondike Lost, Vol. 7, No. 4. Out of print.
Wrangell-Saint Elias, Vol. 8, No. 1. Out of print.
Alaska Mammals, Vol. 8, No. 2. Out of print.
The Kotzebue Basin, Vol. 8, No. 3. Out of print.
Alaska National Interest Lands, Vol. 8, No. 4. $19.95.
*****Alaska's Glaciers**, Vol. 9, No. 1. Rev. 1993. $24.95. Limited.
Sitka and Its Ocean/Island World, Vol. 9, No. 2. Out of print.
Islands of the Seals: The Pribilofs, Vol. 9, No. 3. $9.95.
Alaska's Oil/Gas & Minerals Industry, Vol. 9, No. 4. $9.95.
Adventure Roads North, Vol. 10, No. 1. $9.95.
Anchorage and the Cook Inlet Basin, Vol. 10, No. 2. $19.95.
Alaska's Salmon Fisheries, Vol. 10, No. 3. $9.95.
Up the Koyukuk, Vol. 10, No. 4. $9.95.
Nome, Vol. 11, No. 1. Out of print.
Alaska's Farms and Gardens, Vol. 11, No. 2. $19.95.
Chilkat River Valley, Vol. 11, No. 3. $9.95.
Alaska Steam, Vol. 11, No. 4. $19.95.
Northwest Territories, Vol. 12, No. 1. $9.95.
Alaska's Forest Resources, Vol. 12, No. 2. $9.95.
Alaska Native Arts and Crafts, Vol. 12, No. 3. $24.95.
Our Arctic Year, Vol. 12, No. 4. $19.95.
***** **Where Mountains Meet the Sea**, Vol. 13, No. 1. $19.95.
Backcountry Alaska, Vol. 13, No. 2. $9.95.
British Columbia's Coast, Vol. 13, No. 3. $9.95.
Lake Clark/Lake Iliamna, Vol. 13, No. 4. Out of print.
Dogs of the North, Vol. 14, No. 1. Out of print.
South/Southeast Alaska, Vol. 14, No. 2. $24.95. Limited.
Alaska's Seward Peninsula, Vol. 14, No. 3. $19.95.
The Upper Yukon Basin, Vol. 14, No. 4. $19.95.
Glacier Bay: Icy Wilderness, Vol. 15, No. 1. Out of print.
Dawson City, Vol. 15, No. 2. $19.95.
Denali, Vol. 15, No. 3. $9.95.
The Kuskokwim River, Vol. 15, No. 4. $19.95.
Katmai Country, Vol. 16, No. 1. $19.95.
North Slope Now, Vol. 16, No. 2. $9.95.
The Tanana Basin, Vol. 16, No. 3. $9.95.
***** **The Copper Trail**, Vol. 16, No. 4. $19.95.
***** **The Nushagak Basin**, Vol. 17, No. 1. $19.95.
***** **Juneau**, Vol. 17, No. 2. Out of print.
***** **The Middle Yukon River**, Vol. 17, No. 3. $19.95.
***** **The Lower Yukon River**, Vol. 17, No. 4. $19.95.
***** **Alaska's Weather**, Vol. 18, No. 1. $9.95.
***** **Alaska's Volcanoes**, Vol. 18, No. 2. $24.95. Limited
Admiralty Island: Fortress of Bears, Vol. 18, No. 3. Out of print.
Unalaska/Dutch Harbor, Vol. 18, No. 4. Out of print.
***** **Skagway: A Legacy of Gold**, Vol. 19, No. 1. $9.95.

Alaska: The Great Land, Vol. 19, No. 2. $9.95.
Kodiak, Vol. 19, No. 3. Out of print.
Alaska's Railroads, Vol. 19, No. 4. $19.95.
Prince William Sound, Vol. 20, No. 1. $9.95.
Southeast Alaska, Vol. 20, No. 2. $19.95.
Arctic National Wildlife Refuge, Vol. 20, No. 3. $19.95.
Alaska's Bears, Vol. 20, No. 4. $19.95.
The Alaska Peninsula, Vol. 21, No. 1. $19.95.
The Kenai Peninsula, Vol. 21, No. 2. $19.95.
People of Alaska, Vol. 21, No. 3. $19.95.
Prehistoric Alaska, Vol. 21, No. 4. $19.95.
Fairbanks, Vol. 22, No. 1. $19.95.
The Aleutian Islands, Vol. 22, No. 2. $19.95.
Rich Earth: Alaska's Mineral Industry, Vol. 22, No. 3. $19.95.
World War II in Alaska, Vol. 22, No. 4. $24.95. Limited.
Anchorage, Vol. 23, No. 1. $21.95.
Native Cultures in Alaska, Vol. 23, No. 2. $21.95.
The Brooks Range, Vol. 23, No. 3. $19.95.
Moose, Caribou and Muskox, Vol. 23, No. 4. $19.95.
Alaska's Southern Panhandle, Vol. 24, No. 1. $19.95.
The Golden Gamble, Vol. 24, No. 2. $19.95.
Commercial Fishing in Alaska, Vol. 24, No. 3. $19.95.
Alaska's Magnificent Eagles, Vol. 24, No. 4. $19.95.
Steve McCutcheon's Alaska, Vol. 25, No. 1. $21.95.
Yukon Territory, Vol. 25, No. 2. $21.95.
Climbing Alaska, Vol. 25, No. 3. $21.95.
Frontier Flight, Vol. 25, No. 4. $21.95.
Restoring Alaska: Legacy of an Oil Spill, Vol. 26, No. 1. $21.95.
World Heritage Wilderness, Vol. 26, No. 2. $21.95.
The Bering Sea, Vol. 26, No. 3. $21.95.
Russian America, Vol. 26, No. 4, $21.95.
Best of *ALASKA GEOGRAPHIC*®, Vol. 27, No. 1, $24.95.
Seals, Sea Lions and Sea Otters, Vol. 27, No. 2, $21.95.
Painting Alaska, Vol. 27, No. 3, $21.95.
Living Off the Land, Vol. 27, No. 4, $21.95.
Exploring Alaska's Birds, Vol. 28, No. 1, $23.95.
Glaciers of Alaska, Vol. 28, No. 2, $23.95.
Inupiaq and Yupik People of Alaska, Vol. 28, No. 3, $23.95.
The Iditarod, Vol. 28, No. 4, $23.95.
Secrets of the Aurora Borealis, Vol. 29, No. 1, $23.95.
Boating Alaska, Vol. 29, No. 2, $23.95.
Territory of Alaska, Vol. 29, No. 3, $23.95.
From Kodiak to Unalaska, Vol. 29, No. 4, $23.95.
Alaska's National Wildlife Refuges, Vol. 30, No. 1, $24.95.
Juneau: Yesterday and Today, Vol. 30, No. 2, $24.95.

***** Available in hardback (library binding) — $24.95 each.

PRICES AND AVAILABILITY SUBJECT TO CHANGE